GARDENING UNDER PLASTIC

HOW TO USE FLEECE, FILMS, CLOTHES AND POLYTUNNELS

Bernard Salt

B.T. Batsford Ltd, London

GARDENING UNDER PLASTIC

HOW TO USE FLEECE, FILMS, CLOTHES AND POLYTUNNELS

Bernard Salt

British Library Cataloguing in Publication Data:
A catalogue record for this book is available from the British
Library.

Illustrations have been supplied as follows front cover, frontis-
piece and preface: Garden Answers Magazine, Colin Leftley.
Page 29: Garden Direct. Page 40: Traditional Garden Supply Co.
All other photos, line drawings and diagrams: Bernard Salt.

Acknowledgements:
The author would like to thank Garden Answers Magazine
& Colin Leftley for help with photographic material.
Northern Polytunnels; Defenders Ltd/Wye College; Solar
Tunnels; CLM Fabrications; Growth Technology; First
Tunnels; Phostrogen Ltd.; Miracle Garden Care; Jiffy
Products; Armillatox Ltd.; Link Stakes.

Colour origination by Scanhouse, Malaysia.

Printed in Hong Kong.

Contents

During my lifetime plastic materials have transformed gardening. Plastic gnomes, plastic hose, plastic cans, plastic tubs, plastic pots and plastic protection in the form of cloches, frames, mulches, fleece, nets, wind breaks and polytunnels.

As well as the large range of plastic sheets and fleeces, there is a wonderful variety of cloches and polytunnels available to increase gardening success and enhance enjoyment.

I bought my first polytunnel 14 years ago and it has improved my diet as well as my life. Apart from the two coldest winter months I enjoy gardening all year with the growing season extended at both ends. Polytunnel sheets are now much improved, although not as transparent as glass their ability to retain infra-red is almost as good. They no longer drip and they last much longer. The first sheet I had lasted 4 years whilst my current one is in its seventh year.

Walk into a polytunnel and feel the atmosphere change, experience the different scents, the riot of growth and the freedom from wind and rain. Rake beds, sow seeds, prick out and pot-on whilst the rain lashes down.

I enjoy early potatoes in April, peas, cabbage and cauliflowers in May; lots of peppers, aubergines, cucumbers, melons and tomatoes in summer. A polytunnel is not only about food; I cut chrysanthemums in November, antirrhinums in December, daffodils in February, stocks and sweetpeas in May. In addition my borders are a mass of colour all summer and there are tubs and baskets everywhere, thanks to plants raised under plastic. It rains and blows but whatever the weather I can garden in comfort – what more can anyone ask?

Sadly many gardens are too small to accommodate a polytunnel but this does not prevent the use of cloches and other plastic materials to increase the number and variety of plants. A little ingenuity with a cold frame, a few cloches or a small lean-to structure can produce lots of plants and give hours of enjoyment.

Gardening methods are not written on tablets of stone and there is more than one way of achieving success. The methods I have described here are the ones that have worked for my students and myself. I hope they will also work for you.

Bernard Salt

Chapter One

Protected Cultivation

Inside a domestic polytunnel in July

A polytunnel is very versatile and is used by different gardeners in different ways. The author's polytunnel gives him the following advantages:

- Spring is 6 weeks early.
- Winter is 4 weeks late.
- Delicious food is harvested when it is most expensive in the shops.
- Bedding plants are grown very cheaply.
- Hanging baskets are planted up a month early and in full bloom when hung outside.
- Two crops are raised each year instead of one.
- Tender crops are easily grown.
- Half hardy perennials survive the winter.
- Vegetable yields are higher and the quality is better.
- Flowers are not damaged by wind and storms.
- Fleece placed over plants does not blow away.
- A no-go zone for pigeons and rabbits.
- Carrot flies dislike tunnels.
- Ideal place to raise plants for flowering or cropping outside.
- Conservatory plants are stored during non-flowering periods.
- No heating bills.
- Rain never stops play.

There are of course disadvantages too, these are:
- Daily watering is necessary during the spring and summer months.
- Greenhouse pests such as white fly and red spider mites can be troublesome.
- More skill is required to grow crops in a tunnel than outside.
- The outside appearance is not very aesthetic.

The growing season on these islands is very short, in many areas it is less than 6 months. A 6 week extension of the growing season represents an increase of 25% and this has a dramatic influence on crops and cropping. Plastic sheeting has been developed which gives almost the same 'greenhouse effect' as glass. The 'greenhouse effect' is the term used to explain how a greenhouse acts as a heat trap by letting in the sun's warming rays and preventing the earth's cooling rays from escaping.

Protected cultivation gives freedom from wind chill, hail, snow and rain. The trapped air is not blown away but remains as a warm blanket around the plants. Incidentally the gardener also enjoys these benefits!

The cheapest method of covering an area for plant production is a polytunnel.

A flower border alongside a polytunnel improves its appearance

THE POLYTUNNEL

Every gardener, who has the space, should consider a polytunnel as they give a whole new dimension to gardening. Whatever the weather, polytunnel gardeners can enjoy their hobby to the full. A polytunnel is the cheapest method of protecting the garden and the gardener! A polytunnel will cover four times the area of a greenhouse for a quarter of the price. Contrary to popular belief the covers are tough and good ones will last for 6 years and more.

A polytunnel is not a 'plastic greenhouse'. The management and use of an amateur's greenhouse differs considerably from a polytunnel. A greenhouse is easier to insulate and keep frost free in winter; the light in a greenhouse is a little better than in a polytunnel and a greenhouse is very useful for propagation, especially in early spring when light is at a premium. Ideally a gardener should have both as they are complementary. The author has both; if he had to choose just one, there would be no hesitation – it would be a polytunnel!

A polytunnel consists of a framework of metal hoops, fixed along the top to a metal ridgepole. In some polytunnels the hoops are shaped to give vertical sides. This shape is recommended where tunnel widths are less than 5m (16ft).

The frame is covered with a single sheet of polythene, secured to wooden door frames at each end. The doors double as ventilators. One advantage a tunnel has over a greenhouse is that the design of the end is easily varied. The author recommends fitting double doors at each end to provide both good access and good ventilation.

Siting

In most gardens the chosen site will be a compromise between what is ideal and what is practical. The following must all be considered:

1. Light – avoid deep shade, this is of extreme importance especially in the winter and early spring. A tunnel with the ridge running east-west will receive more sun than one with the ridge running north-south.
2. Access – easy access from the house to the tunnel and a good surface on the path will probably lead to better care for the plants.
3. Aesthetic – 'beauty is in the eye of the beholder' but in most peoples' eyes a polytunnel is not very good to look at.
4. Trees – these should not shade nor overhang the polytunnel but, when far enough away, make good wind breaks.
5. Distance from the boundary – a clear area of at least 1.2m (4ft) around the polytunnel is almost essential when fixing the cover. This space need not be wasted as it may provide a useful area for standing boxes of plants.
6. Wind – shelter from cold prevailing winds helps to keep the temperature up. A gap between two buildings will sometimes create a wind tunnel. Such situations should be avoided.
7. Foundations are not a problem with polytunnels, a level site has many advantages and every effort should be made to achieve this.
8. Soil – good and free draining is ideal, poor soil can be overcome by creating raised beds inside the polytunnel and filling them with good topsoil.
9. Frost – frost pockets or hollows should be avoided where possible.

Services

1. Water supply – a tap inside a polytunnel is virtually essential for tunnels of 50m² (538ft²) and above.
2. Electricity supply – is not essential but very useful for lighting, heating a propagator and operating other equipment such as a shredder. This must be installed by a certified electrician and all equipment protected with a residual current device.

Erecting A Polytunnel

Polytunnels are usually supplied in kit form and the erection is easy for the average handy person, but (unless the tunnel is very small) four people are needed to attach the cover. After the tunnel has arrived the first job is to lay out and identify all the parts.

Marking Out The Base

1. Using two pegs and a length of string mark the position of the tunnel side. Drive in the pegs 1m (3ft) or so beyond each end of the tunnel and tie the string taut between them.

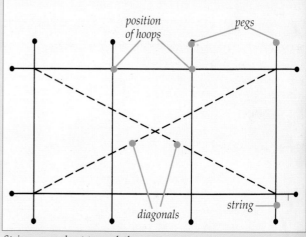

Strings pegged out to mark the exact position of the foundation tubes

2. Mark both ends in the same way, squaring the corners with a rectangle of wood or a 3-4-5 triangle.
3. Fix the line that marks the other side. You now have eight pegs and four pieces of string. The points where the strings cross mark the corners of the tunnel.
4. Measure both diagonals, if the measurements are not exactly the same, the base is not square. If necessary, adjust the strings until the diagonals are exactly the same length, this is most important.
5. Mark the positions of the ends of intermediate hoops with pegs and string. The distances between the hoops should be equal.
6. Leave the pegs where they are and remove the strings.
7. Dig the holes.

Fixing hoops

After the concrete has set, the sequence of erection is as follows:
1. Slide the hoops into position.
2. Fix the ridgepole with the brackets provided but do not tighten any nuts.
3. Adjust the hoops, by raising and lowering them into the sockets, until they are vertical and exactly in line with each other.
4. Tighten all nuts.
5. Fix the door frames by concreting the bases into the ground and fixing the tops to the end hoops with the clips that are supplied.
6. Cover all nuts and sharp edges with adhesive tape.
7. Stick anti-hotspot tape over the outside of the hoops. Anti-hotspot tape is very smooth which helps the positioning of the sheet; it also extends the life of a polythene cover by at least one year. This tape is usually supplied as an optional extra. In the author's opinion it is essential.

8. Fill the holes with concrete and replace the strings. Push the tubes, which are to hold the hoops into the wet concrete. The tubes must be vertical and their centres exactly underneath the point where the strings cross.
9. Using a long straight plank and a spirit level check that the tops of the tubes are level; drive in any which are proud. (Note: protect the top of the tube with a board before hitting it with a hammer).

Covering The Tunnel

Different manufacturers have different methods of fixing the sheet. Points to remember are:
1. Wait for a calm day as the slightest breeze makes a cover unmanageable. The air is most still at dawn and this may be a suitable time to cover the frame.
2. If the plastic is treated on one side with an anti-fogging agent make sure you put it on the right side up. Always follow the manufacturers' instructions.

A solar tunnel frame ready for sheeting up

An anti-fogging treatment causes droplets of condensation to spread into a thin film. This prevents drips, allows more light in and improves insulation.

3. When pulling the sheet taut, take care not to stretch it.

4. Lay the sheet out along one side of the tunnel with an equal amount at each end.

5. Drag the sheet over the tunnel and adjust to make the overlap at the sides equal.

6. Make two vertical cuts at one end, to allow for the door, 30cm (1ft) less than the width of the door.

7. Allow 60cm (2ft) for fixing and cut off surplus plastic that would otherwise cover the door.

8. Take a wooden batten, the width of the door frame, and roll the plastic that is hanging below the door frame around it.

9. Use galvanised nails to fix the wood (with plastic wrapped around) to the outside face of the top of the frame.

10. Repeat the operations at the other end. Before nailing in position pull the sheet as tight as possible along the length of the ridge, the final appearance of the tunnel depends upon this.

11. Beginning in the middle and working towards the ends, fix the sheet along each side, pulling out any creases and getting it as taut as possible. The sides of the sheet are either buried in the ground or fixed to special horizontal rails.

If using rails fix them to the hoops about 20cm (8in) above their final position; when the sheet is attached to the rails push down hard and tighten the nuts. Bury the surplus sheet to form a draught proof seal.

12. Pull the sheet around the end hoop as tightly and crease-free as possible. Fix the sheet to the sides of the door frame by nailing on wooden battens.

13. Hang the doors.

14. Cover the doors with surplus plastic. A staple gun is the best tool for this purpose, double the plastic over to form 'washers'.

A 14ft wide polytunnel

Ventilation

Ventilation is provided by opening doors or vents at both ends of a polytunnel. Apart from cold spells in the depth of winter, one end (or sometimes both) should be opened every day. This is most important in autumn when conditions become favourable for grey mould and other fungus diseases. On sunny days which are followed by frosty nights the tunnel should be ventilated by day but closed up an hour or so before the sun goes down. A layer of condensation then forms on the inside of the sheet, this freezes and gives additional insulation.

A polytunnel should always be given maximum ventilation by day during the summer. It is best to close up in the evening to keep the night time temperature as high as possible. A large difference between day and night temperatures can cause problems – especially with tomatoes.

In winter, during very cold spells, keep the polytunnel closed both day and night.

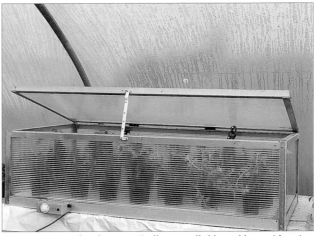

A propagator, with a thermostatically controlled heated base with twin wall polycarbonate top, is a cost effective method of raising plants early in the growing season

Temperature

A polytunnel warms by the greenhouse effect, much of this warmth remains as there is little chill factor from the wind. It is unheated and the temperature inside will fall below freezing. Closing up well before sundown in spring and autumn is an essential part of tunnel management. Tender crops such as early potatoes are best covered with fleece. This will not need anchoring as there is no wind to blow it away. In very cold spells a body blanket (aluminium foil) can be used as a second cover during night time only.

In summer a polytunnel can become very hot even when doors and vents are fully open. Plants withstand these high temperatures providing the air is humid and they are well watered.

A frame made of polystyrene sheets and a polycarbonate top. This is used inside a polytunnel to protect the most tender plants during severe weather

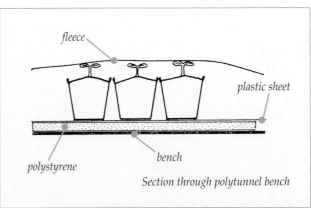

fleece

plastic sheet

polystyrene

bench

Section through polytunnel bench

The polytunnel bench in May

potting, taking cuttings, etc. The height of staging should be adjusted to a comfortable working height by placing bricks under the legs. The area underneath is a good place to grow chrysanthemum stools, dahlia tubers for cuttings, ferns and shade tolerant plants. It is not a good place to store used boxes and pots.

An average handy person could produce home made benches from a variety of materials. Care should be taken however not to provide nooks and crannies that may encourage pests and diseases. Wooden benches are better when covered with a sheet of white plastic. This is easy to clean, reflects light and looks good. All benches and staging should be level. This is very important for a capillary bed or it will not function properly.

The same bench in winter

Inside Organisation

Once the polytunnel is complete the inside will need to be organised. It is better to have the path down the length of the polytunnel off centre to allow the ridgepole to be used for plant support and/or hanging baskets. The polytunnel in the photographs is organised into a number of 1m (4ft) wide raised beds with wooden surrounds. There is 1m (3ft 6in) benching along one side with a path running the full length between the beds and the bench.

The bench consists of old tables, purchased cheaply from a scrap merchant. The tables are covered with white plastic sheeting; this is clean and hygienic, it also reflects light.

Staging

Staging helps to organise a polytunnel into a convenient production unit, with places for pot and tray grown plants. A slatted top allows air to flow around the plants. This helps to control fungus diseases in autumn but in summer it makes plants dry out more quickly. A solid top gives a good working area for sowing,

Plant Support

The ridgepole provides a good place for hanging baskets and for attaching strings or nets for plant support.

A useful method of providing other anchor points is to run a wire, complete with strainer, along the length of the polytunnel and attach it to the wooden uprights which form the door posts. Strings from this wire to the ridgepole provide intermediate anchor points.

A strainer holds the plant supporting wire taut. The wire runs the length of the tunnel and is used as an anchor for plant supports

Choosing A Polytunnel

When selecting a polytunnel there are four golden rules:

1. Make certain that the hoops are strong enough to withstand snow loading. Steel hoops galvanised inside and out are ideal. In addition the structure is stronger if the hoops are no more than 2.4m (8ft) apart.

2. Choose a wide tunnel rather than a narrow one. A short wide polytunnel is better than a long narrow one both for working space and for ventilation.

3. Make sure that there is a clearance of 1m (3ft) on both sides and the far end of the tunnel.

4. Choose the best available sheet and one that is treated with an anti-fogging agent. The extra cost will be more than repaid by longer life and greater energy efficiency. The anti-fogging agent also prevents annoying drips of water down the gardener's neck and (more important) harmful drips of water onto the plants.

In addition to the 'standard' polytunnel there are more sophisticated ones available for amateur gardeners. These are all excellent in their way with advantages over the standard ones. They are also more expensive.

Solar Tunnel

Inside a polytunnel

A solar tunnel is best described as a hybrid between a polytunnel and a greenhouse. The sides are vertical and the roof domed. The cover is PVC reinforced with a green 1cm sq mesh. The green appearance and vertical sides make a solar tunnel a more attractive addition to a garden than a standard polytunnel. A solar tunnel is secured with large corkscrew anchor bolts. These can be unscrewed from the ground and the whole structure carried to a new site. This operation needs four strong (or six not so strong) people. Unlike the standard polytunnel the sheeting is supplied in pieces. Each piece has its edge folded over and welded to form a continuous loop. 'Draw strings' threaded through the loops are used to hold the sheets in position. It is possible (but not desirable) to erect a solar tunnel in a fairly strong wind.

Solar tunnels are available in 3 and 4m (10 and 13ft) widths and any length. The cost is more than a polytunnel and less than a greenhouse. ☎ *01903 742615 for a catalogue.*

John Walker, the well-known garden expert, is a solar tunnel enthusiast

The solar tunnel, with its green appearance, fits well into the garden design

Keder House

A Keder house is covered with a type of plastic very similar to the large bubble plastic that is available as a greenhouse insulator. It is very strong, the bubbles are virtually unbreakable and a roof section will carry the weight of three people. Keder plastic is half the cost of glass with double the insulation properties. Manufactured in 2m (6ft) wide sheets, the edge of the sheet has a continuous cylinder that fits into a

A Keder midihouse. Smaller Keder houses are also available

female plastic strip. This strip is fixed to galvanised steel supports by means of self tapping coach bolts. Many commercial growers now use Keder plastic and a firm in Malvern is supplying 'midi houses' with this type of sheeting. Apart from the additional insulation qualities offered by the

Keder plastic, these houses have excellent side ventilation - a real boon in the summer and autumn. The delivered and erected price of a 4x8m (13x26ft) midi house is around £2,000 which is much more than a standard polytunnel but much less than the traditional greenhouse. ☎ *01386 49094 for a catalogue.*

Planning Permission?

Regulations are subject to change. At the time of writing, domestic greenhouses and small polytunnels are not subject to planning. It is always worthwhile checking with your local planning department, especially if you are in a conservation area.

What To Grow?

Polytunnels have many different uses including housing animals, growing mushrooms, protecting fishponds, shading houses, staging exhibitions, covering swimming pools and of course growing plants.

The last item begs the question, 'what plants?' and the answer is 'Any type of plant the owner wishes to grow'.

In practice there are plants that thrive in a polytunnel and others that grow as well outside.

> **Basically most domestic polytunnels are used to:**
> - extend the growing season.
> - propagate plants.
> - protect less hardy plants in winter.
> - grow plants from warmer climates in summer.
> - produce food for the family.
> - produce cut flowers for the house.
> - raise plants for the vegetable garden.
> - raise half hardy annuals for the flower borders.
> - propagate hardy perennials for flower borders.
> - store conservatory plants that are not in flower.
> - allow the gardener to enjoy his/her hobby regardless of the weather.

Which types of plants are grown or protected varies according to the interests and circumstances of the polytunnel owner. Some polytunnels are packed to overflowing in winter and used less in summer and others are bursting in summer and virtually empty in winter. The author's polytunnel is full throughout the year. Listed on the page opposite, season by season, are the plants that flourish. For clarity each item is included only once, many obviously overlap the seasons.

Spring

Vegetables for harvesting
cabbage
carrots
cauliflower
cress
lettuce
potatoes
radish
spinach
strawberry

Flowers for cutting
sweet william
brompton stocks
spring bulbs
sweet peas
gypsophila

*Plants being raised
from seeds for growing
elsewhere*
many bedding plants
most vegetables
pot plants
conservatory plants

*Plants being grown
from cuttings or bulbs*
hanging basket plants
conservatory plants
patio plants

Summer

Fruit for harvesting
aubergines
pepper
tomatoes
melons

Vegetables for harvesting
sweetcorn
courgettes

*Plants being raised
from seeds for growing
elsewhere*
hardy biennials and
hardy perennials

*Plants being grown
from cuttings or bulbs*
house plants
coleus
exacum
achimenes

Autumn

Vegetables for harvesting
sweetcorn

Flowers for cutting
antirrhinum
gomphrena
chrysanthemums

*Plants being raised
from seeds for growing
elsewhere*
endive

*Plants being grown
from cuttings or bulbs*
half hardy 'stock'
plants for hanging
baskets and
tubs
many shrubs
slightly tender
perennials
e.g. penstemon

Winter

Vegetables for harvesting
chicory
endive
parsley
carrot

Flowers for cutting
chrysanthemums

*Plants being raised
from seeds for growing
elsewhere*
sweetpeas
broad beans
onions

*Plants being protected
from winter cold*
patio plants in tubs
e.g. myrtle, slightly
tender perennials
e.g. lobelia cardinalis

A Keder House

In the depths of winter nothing actually grows as the temperature and light levels are too low. During this time the polytunnel is used as a 'holding operation' by keeping plants in readiness for warmer and lighter days.

CROPPING PLAN *season by season*

WINTER (JANUARY)

On the bench in pots

Strawberries
(brought in week 3)
Sweet peas in
root trainers
(sown November)
Polyanthus
(sown July)

Rooted cuttings of:
hardy perennials
(taken last summer)
Broad beans in
root trainers
(sown week 1 germinated
in propagator)

with additional protection

Half hardy perennials
for cuttings for tubs
and baskets– bidens
surfinia, Swedish ivy,
margarites, helichrysum–
(taken last summer)

In the heated propagator

Germinating seeds of:
Geranium
Lobelia
Begonias
Onions
Parsley
Hispi cabbage

Parsley
(cropping)

Brompton Stocks
(planted from pots
in October)

Land cress
(sown
week 4)

Endive
(cropping)

Lettuce
(Kelly's
planted
December)

Chrysanthemum
stools in
large pots
(plunged)

Half hardy
shrubs with extra
protection
(in patio tubs)

Sweet Williams
(planted from pots
in October)

Spring bulbs for
cutting (planted
in October)

Dug and manured

Dug and manured

SPRING (APRIL)

**On the bench in pots,
trays and, root trainers**

Strawberries (in flower)
lettuce, cauliflower
cabbage, fennel, parsley,
cabbage, Brussels sprouts,
onions, leeks (for planting
outside weeks 3 & 4)

**With fleece cover at
night in frosty weather**

Chrysanthemum &
dahlia cuttings.
Trays of various bedding
plants. Tomato &
aubergine plants.
Plants for hanging
baskets (baskets planted
up week 4 and hung on
ridge pole)

Runner beans, sweet corn
& French beans in root
trainers

Marrows
Courgettes

In the heated propagator

Seeds of bedding plants

Seeds of pot plants

Cucumbers

Parsley
(cropping)

Brompton Stocks
in flower

(whole bed cleared, dug
and manured week 4)

Lettuce
(being harvested)

Spinach (sown
February week 1,
being harvested)

(whole bed cleared, dug
and manured week 4)

Early Potatoes
(planted February week 2
harvested throughout May)

Sweet Williams
(cut during May)

Courgettes (extra
protection in frosty
weather, crop all
summer)

Early carrots &
spring onions
(sown February
week 2, harvested
May-August

Beetroot
(transplanted,
harvested May)

Hispi cabbage
(planted March,
harvested
weeks 3 & 4)

Cauliflower
(planted March,
harvested May)

(Sweet peas on the edge of three
plots for cutting in May & June)

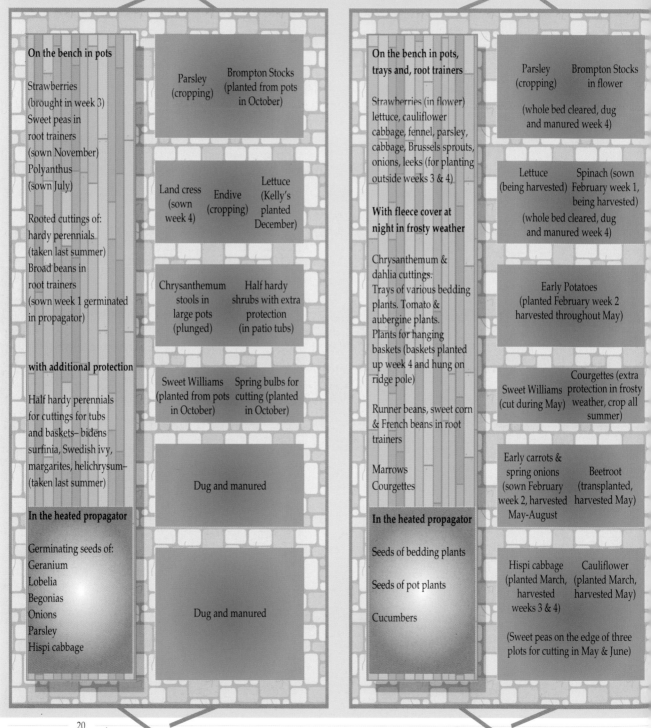

SUMMER (JULY)

On the bench in various containers

Cuttings of half hardy perennials taken from tubs and baskets

Pot plants from seeds e.g. coleus, asparagus, spanish flag, basil

Trays of pansies, Canterbury bells, polyanthus, fox gloves and other biennials ready for potting on

Sweet Williams Brompton Stocks (grown individually in 12.5cm [5in] pots)

In the heated propagator

Cuttings of half hardy plants and house plants.

Whole bed of tomatoes (crop July-November)

Whole bed of tomatoes (crop July-November)

Antirrhinums (for December cut flowers)

Sweet corn (planted May week 3, ready August)

Melons (planted June week 1) (harvest Aug/Sept)

Courgettes (cropping)

Carrots (harvesting)

Carrots (sown June for winter crop)

Parsley (sown July for winter/spring crop)

Cucumber, aubergines, peppers (planted May for summer crop)

AUTUMN (OCTOBER)

On the bench in pots

Rooted cuttings of hardy perennials

Sweet peas germinating (just a few for flowering inside the tunnel – more will be sown later for outside flowering)

Polyanthus Pansies

Ranuculus corms to provide cut flowers in March

with additional protection

Rooted half hardy cuttings of perennials for tubs and baskets

In the heated propagator

Cuttings of various tender house plants. (Begonia Rex, Saint Paulia etc.)

Tomatoes – cropping until the first severe frosts. Bed dug and manured immediately upon crop removal

Tomatoes – cropping until the first severe frosts. Bed dug and manured immediately upon crop removal

Antirrhinums for cutting in December

Radish spring onions (winter hardy)

Endive

Chrysanthemums in large pot in flower. (Protect late blooms from frost with fleece)

Sweet Williams Carrots

Parsley Brompton Stocks

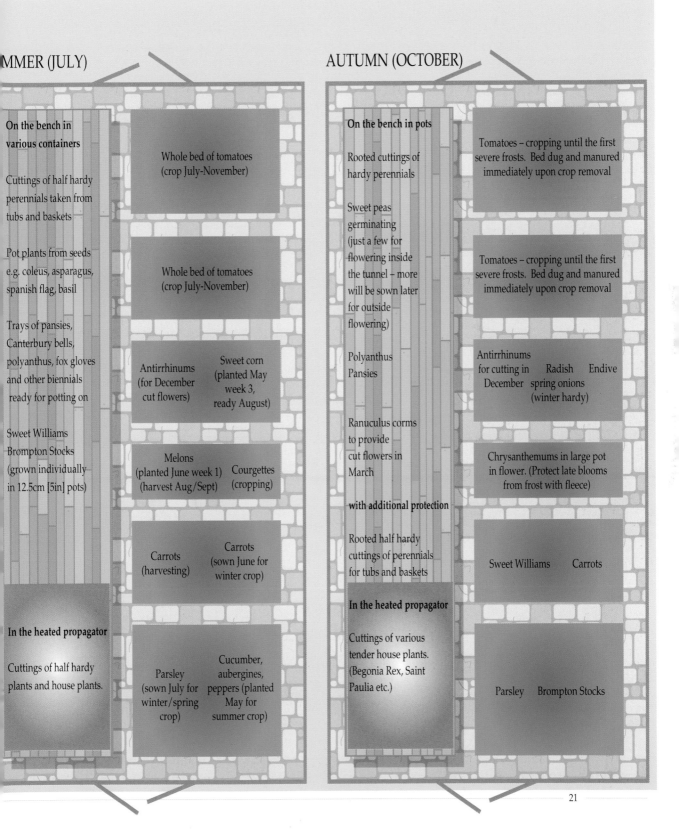

21

CLOCHES

A cloche is a low transparent cover that is designed to protect large plants during the early stages of their growth and small plants from sowing to maturity. They come in many shapes and sizes. Some are expensive, rigid and easy to use, whilst others are cheap, flimsy and time consuming.

Cloches are most useful in spring when they warm the soil and protect crops during germination and early growth. Cloches are useful in autumn for late sown crops and in winter to protect vegetables such as carrots and flowers such as anemones. Some cloche manufacturers recommend grow-

Small Melbourne cloche covering two rows of lettuce

Care is necessary when removing cloche protection or plants may suffer a severe check. A gradual increase in ventilation during the 1 or 2 weeks before complete cloche removal will avoid damage. The time taken depends upon

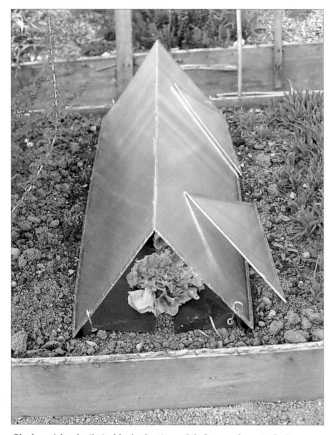

Cloche with a built in black plastic mulch for weed control. An effective cloche with difficult access

ing melons, aubergines and cucumbers under cloches throughout the summer. These plants often become too large to be accommodated under cloches, leaves scorch and fungus diseases spread with alarming rapidity. There are exceptions, but the best place for most cloches at the height of summer is the garden shed.

Cloche being used to grow a few lettuces in a flower garden

the weather. Dull damp days are better for cloche removal than sunny ones as, when the covers are off, the plants are subjected to reduced humidity as well as lower temperatures.

A few good cloches are an excellent garden aid and have the following uses:

- Warming the soil in early spring to bring forward sowing and planting dates.
- Help transplants to become established.
- Protect plants from birds, rabbits and some insects.
- Enable half hardy crops to be grown by protecting them during the early stages of growth.
- Protect from late spring frost.
- Harden off greenhouse and polytunnel grown plants.
- Covering parts of rows of salads to stagger maturity times.
- As a nursery area for brassica, lettuce and other plants.
- Protect some crops throughout the winter.
- Protect alpines from winter rain – fully ventilated.
- Covering anemones in winter to obtain early cut flowers.
- Protect autumn sown hardy annuals such as cornflowers, larkspur, sweet peas etc. throughout the winter.
- Extend the season into late autumn for parsley, lettuce etc.
- Protect cuttings of hardy perennials throughout the winter.
- Warm soil and protect seedlings of hardy annuals.
- Warm soil and protect from frost the early growth of new potatoes.
- Warm the soil in early spring for sowing (or planting) lettuce, spring onions etc.

- Warm the soil for planting early cabbage etc.
- Cover strawberries to protect the flowers from frost and have an earlier crop with no bird damage.
- Harden off French and runner bean plants that have been raised in a polytunnel.
- Protect overwintering lettuce, broad beans, Japanese onions and salad onions.
- Protect pea seedlings from birds.
- Cover herbs e.g. mint in late winter to obtain an early spring supply.
- Prevent birds and cats from eating slug pellets.

Limitations of Cloches
- The night temperature is only a degree or so above the outside temperature and plants can become frost damaged.
- Plants may become tender and collapse when the cloche is removed.
- Leaves and growing points that are in contact with the plastic are sometimes damaged.
- An increased possibility of fungus diseases.
- With some types of cloche watering is difficult
- Weed germination and growth is speeded up.

Note: This list is a guide to possibilities only and is not intended to be complete.

Points To Remember When Using Cloches

When properly used, cloches are a real boon for flower, salad and vegetable crops especially in the spring. To get full benefit from soil warming in spring, cloches must be in place for at least 2 weeks before sowing. Sudden removal should be avoided as plants may collapse in wind or sun. Some cloches are designed to allow for a gradual increase in ventilation but many are not. Plants can be gradually acclimatised to outside conditions by removing the cloches during the day and replacing them at night. In hot weather this may be preceded by removing the cloches for a few hours in the evening for 2 or 3 days.

Ultimate cloche

Solar Bell

Weslon polythene cloche

Cloches Available

The Ultimate Cloche

from Klik-A-Stick Ltd (Tel. 0121 344 4040)

A frameless cloche made from twin wall polycarbonate. One metre long and half a metre wide, with good headroom. It hinges on two ground pins to give easy access. It has two adjustable vents. Water by simply clipping on a hose. The integral watering system consists of two atomisers with a universal hose connection.

Author's Verdict:

This cloche gives excellent results. The watering sytem allows salads to be produced in warm weather when crops in other cloches might possibly scorch. To economize on water, the hose should be fitted with a stop end. Useful in a polytunnel as a mist propagator for rooting cuttings.

Solar Bell

from Haxnicks (☎ 01585 233973)

A vacuum formed plastic dome, reminiscent of the Victorian glass bells. Four pre-drilled holes in the base for anchorage (anchor pegs not supplied). Ventilation by tilting and raising one side from the ground. Shaped to prevent condensation from dripping onto plants.

Author's verdict:

I have used bells in the past and find condensation to be a problem. This is a cheap product for which a knowledgeable gardener would have many uses, and a lot of success. It is also ideal for the novice gardener to make mistakes with, and learn from.

Weslon Polythene Cloche

from Marshalls (☎ 01945 583407)

An ingenious method of converting a polythene tube into a tunnel cloche. Just two simple steps and the cloche is assembled. Six tunnels per pack and two end closures produces a tunnel 15ft (4.5m) long. The end closure consists of a polythene bag pulled over an open ended rectangle of wire. All the wires protrude 10cm (4in) to push into the ground for anchorage.

Author's verdict:

A cheap alternative to rigid plastic. It will be effective, but not very good looking. It is okay for use on the allotment or out of sight in the vegetable garden.

Clever-Cloche
from Agralan (☎ 01285 860015)

A slightly opaque corrugated plastic sheet with pre-drilled holes is cut into a shape which forms four different types of plant protection. The instructions are very good and all four shapes are very easy to achieve.

Barn shape: The traditional cloche shape – just large enough to take a standard grow bag. The cloche is anchored by sliding three pegs through the side and under the growbag. Two semicircular ventilators in the top section provides good adjustable ventilation. The vents also give access for watering.

Shelter shape: When the growbag crop becomes too tall for the barn shape, clever-cloche opens to form a 'lean-to' and protects plants growing against a wall.

Box shape: The substitution of one end bolt for two and using different holes, the barn becomes a box. Two roof vents provide good ventilation.

Spread shape: This is the box with the sides splayed out giving slightly more ground cover. The four anchor pins provided are unlikely to prevent a strong wind from blowing clever-cloche away when used in this mode.

Author's verdict:
Some clever ideas here – especially with the ventilation. Cloches are most useful at the times of the year when light levels are low, this makes me think that the opaqueness of the material must be a disadvantage. The box shape is a useful small cold frame.

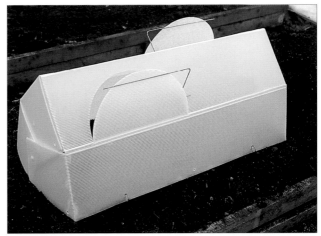
Clever cloche

Enviromesh Tunnel Kit
from Agralan (☎ 01285 860015)

This kit consists of a piece of insect netting 1.8mx4.5m (6ftx15ft) and four plastic hoops. The hoops are pushed into the ground to form a tunnel 3.6m (12ft) long. The net is draped over and the edges buried in the ground. If properly cleaned and stored the net will last for 5 years.

Author's verdict:
This 'cloche' is marketed as a protection against insect pests of vegetables. It will certainly do that, it will also give some protection against wind and storm damage. The hoops are plastic and should last for ever. However, they are so flimsy the cloche is virtually impossible to assemble. If you want safe food and a garden full of wildlife throw your sprays away and use insect netting with better hoops.

Enviromesh tunnel

County Cloche
from Kings Seeds (☎ 01376 570000)

This consists of a 1m (4ft) sheet of clear corrugated plastic firmly held in a tunnel shape by two plastic injection mouldings. The mouldings are joined with a metal alloy rod that doubles as a handle. The ends of the tunnel are

County cloche

Super cloche

Barn cloche clips, designed for glass but being used here with polycarbonate

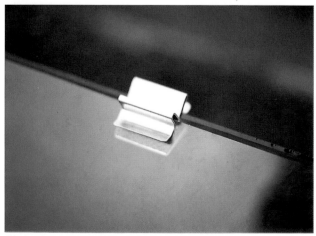
Cloche clips

sealed by two clear plastic sheets, shaped for the purpose. Ventilation is obtained by off-setting the end covers. This cloche is also available in 2 and 4m 6.5 and 12ft lengths. The longer ones consist of two (or three) 1m (3ft) ones with just two end closures. Good suggestions for use including an all the year round sowing guide.

Author's verdict:

Sturdy, effective and easy to use. A sensibly sized cloche that will last at least 10 years. When not in use it will store flat and can be reassembled in seconds. Good value for money.

Super Cloche
from Agriframes ☎ (01342) 328644

This cloche uses a similar sheet of corrugated clear PVC to the Kings County Cloche but the method of support and ventilation is entirely different. All the edges of the plastic are protected with galvanised steel and the central steel support doubles as a handle. Both ends are ventilated with a 'hit and miss' circle overlapping holes in the end. Instructions are very clear and easy to follow.

Author's verdict:

An excellent cloche which looks 'smart' in use – a pity the ventilation holes are not larger.

Chase Barn Cloche Fittings
from Power Garden Products (☎ 01676 523062)

The pack contained four strong wires, formed into various shapes. The wires hold four sheets of glass in a 'barn' shape which gives good clearance over the plants. One of the roof sheets can be held in a raised position for ventilation, or removed to allow access to the crop. The weight of the glass makes the cloche heavy enough to make anchoring unnecessary. The glass can be cut from standard 5x5cm (2ftx2in) sheets of horticultural glass with no wastage. Two sizes of this cloche are available, each covers the same area but one is 30cm (12in) high and the other is 48cm (19in) high. The instructions are well illustrated and easy to follow. A useful sowing guide is included.

Author's verdict:

An excellent buy for any gardener who has spare panes of glass. This type of cloche has been tried and tested over many years. They are best used, placed end to end to form a tunnel, each end of which is covered with a sheet of glass. No mention is made of the fact that glass may have sharp edges – wear gloves when assembling these cloches. Better still, use polycarbonate instead of glass, the cloche can then be made twice as long, but it will need anchoring.

Rumsey Cloche Clips
from G R S Eng. Co., Storrington, West Sussex, RH20 3EA

A strong metal clip with a non-slip surface designed to hold two panes of glass at right angles to form a tent cloche. The clip also forms a handle. Two additional pieces of glass are needed to cover the ends.

Author's verdict:
I used these many years ago – they are very good for warming soil, germinating seeds or a single row of lettuce. In common with other cloches of this shape many plants soon grow out of them. A good way of putting idle sheets of glass to work.

Melbourne Cloche
from Jemp (☎ 01753 548327)

This cloche consists of a very strong plastic sheet, with automatic ventilation flaps. This is held taut and rigid by a tubular metal frame that threads through loops welded into the cover. The ends are closed by clipping on two shaped plastic sheets. One cloche can be used on its own or several can be placed end to end to form a tunnel. Pegs are supplied to tether against the wind.

Author's verdict:
This is the Rolls Royce of cloches. I have used two for years, as covers over large propagators and in the garden for general crop production. Three different widths are available, all are 150cm (5ft) long. The 1m (3ft) one is an excellent size as it is the same width as a soil bed. My garden is in a very windy situation and I have not had to use the tethers.

Maxi Cloche
from Hortissentials Ltd (☎ 01282 866778)

A curved twin wall polycarbonate sheet held by moulded plastic ends and legs.

Author's verdict:
An excellent and easy to use cloche. The ventilation is inadequate but easily corrected by cutting a larger hole and covering it with fleece.

Barn Cloche
from Hortissentials Ltd (☎ 01282 866778)

Twin wall polycarbonate sheets held into a barn shape by very strong metal hoops. Useful handles incorporated into the hoops. Ends held by two garden canes (supplied).

Author's verdict:
A real good cloche, a sensible size, very versatile and very useful. Competes with the Melbourne cloche for the Rolls Royce logo!

Melbourne cloche

Maxi cloche

Barn cloche

Floating Mulches

A floating mulch is a layer of plastic or fleece laid over a crop and held in place by burying the edges in soil. If raised beds, with wooden surrounds are used, the mulch can be fixed to the wood by means of a staple gun.

Horticultural Fleece

There are many references to 'fleece' or 'horticultural fleece' throughout this book, an indication of how useful this material is. Horticultural fleece is probably the gardeners' best aid for additional crop protection.

Fleece is a fabric made from polypropylene. The polypropylene is stabilised against ultra violet light and formed into a mass of short threads. The threads are not woven together like normal cloth, but pressed together in a higgledy-piggledy fashion. The result is a very light material that can lie on top of plants without harming them. Plants grow well underneath as it admits light, air and water. The parts of plants that are in direct contact with the material do not become damaged as may happen with film.

Fleece is superior to plastic sheets because of its lightness and its ability to 'breathe'. Unlike plastic film, fleece need not be removed but can remain over the plants until they mature. In addition, plants protected by fleece are much less likely to suffer from the wind damage and scorch associated with films.

Cabbage and cauliflower protected from cabbage root fly, rabbits and pigeons by a single layer of fleece stapled to the raised bed surround

A fleece cloche is easily made by stapling a 2m (2yd) length between two roof laths the length of which is equal to the width of the fleece. The cloche is reduced or extended by winding or unwinding fleece around one of the laths. The laths are placed either side of a row and are usually heavy enough to prevent the fleece from blowing away. A peg or brick on the laths will only be necessary in very windy areas.

Apart from giving protection from the weather, a fleece cloche protects brassica plants from cabbage root fly, cabbage aphid, rabbits, pigeons, cabbage moth and cabbage butterflies.

Inside a polytunnel on a frosty night in March

Fleece, stapled onto a frame made of tile laths, to protect chrysanthemum plants from the wind

Fleece protecting newly transplanted runner bean plants from the wind

Horticultural fleece is invaluable inside a polytunnel for covering plants as additional frost protection. Here the fleece does not need anchoring against wind and placing it over the plants takes only a few seconds. When used outside, fleece tends to become dirty and torn towards the end of the season. When used inside a polytunnel it will last for many seasons.

Plastic Film

Transparent plastic sheeting with either slits or holes at close and regular intervals is also used as a mulch. It is laid on the soil and held by burying the edges. In spring the sheet is applied 2 or 3 weeks before the crop is sown. The effect of the sheet is to warm the soil a degree or two and to retain soil moisture by reducing evaporation. A good deal more skill is needed with plastic film than with fleece. The humidity under film is usually much higher than the surrounding air.

Plastic shading used as a windbreak

Great care is needed with timing the removal of the sheet, otherwise the crop may collapse. Leaves can suffer sun scorch especially if they are in direct contact with the plastic.

Opaque Mulches

Black plastic sheeting is used in the following ways:

Laid over a neglected area to kill weeds by excluding light. This is very effective but can take a long time (over a year) for perennials such as convolvulus (bindweed) and brambles. The time can be reduced by spraying the weeds with glyphosate (sold as Tumbleweed or Roundup) before covering. The glyphosate is most effective when the weeds are actively growing.

In the form of a collar around the base of a tree. This prevents weed growth by the trunk and reduces evaporation of soil water.

Where a new hedge is to be planted, a strip of black plastic is first laid down and the hedging plants are then planted through it. This removes the need for weeding and the hedge establishes more quickly. If the plastic is thought to be unsightly it can be covered with coarse bark chips.

Other Uses Of Plastic In The Garden

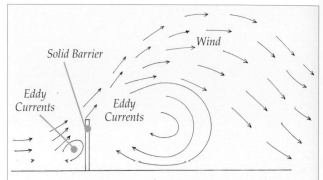

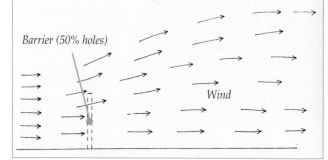

Eddy currents are worse for plants than direct wind. A perforated barrier however reduces wind by 70% and causes no eddy currents.

'Terratex' mulch replaces straw on a bed of strawberries

Windbreaks

The prevailing wind in most parts of the UK is from the south and west, in some areas (and some gardens) the prevailing wind is from a different direction due to the effects of hills and/or buildings. In many parts of the country winds from the east and the north are the most damaging.

Solid windbreaks do not work. This is because they cause eddy currents on both sides of the structure. Trees are planted as windbreaks but this is not a practical option in most gardens – the roots can block drains and trees compete with garden plants for water. In the garden temporary plastic windbreaks can be very effective. Vertical barriers are easily erected around a susceptible crop. A frame made of tile laths with plastic netting stapled on is all that is required in a vegetable or fruit garden. In windy areas a structure like this around a strawberry bed will increase the yield by up to 50%. The appearance of a structure such as this is probably not acceptable in a flower garden. Gardens that have a serious wind problem may benefit from a permanent fence of 5cm (2in) plastic strips fixed horizontally 5cm (2in) apart. These are manufactured by 'Growing Technologies' (☎ 0115 9551313 for the nearest stockist). This type of windbreak reduces wind speeds of 22mph down to just 7mph. A cheaper, but not as permanent alternative, is Rokolene windbreak shade (50% shade value). This and similar products are available off the roll in a number of large garden centres.

Plastic Ground Cover

Woven black plastic materials designed as ground cover. Two of the better known makes are 'Terratex' and 'MyPex'. These are used in the horticultural industry to form a clean surface upon which to stand container and pot plants. This material prevents soil erosion and weed growth. It also forms a clean working surface. Water seeps through the weave and prevents puddling. It has several garden uses. In the polytunnel it can be used to cover a soil bed in order to create a temporary standing area for pots. The photograph on the opposite page shows 'Terratex' in use as a permanent strawberry mulch. Weeds are suppressed and the fruit is protected from rain-splash. At fruiting time the bed is covered with fleece to protect the crop from birds and allows slug pellets to be used safely.

Cold Frames

A cold frame differs from a cloche in shape and size - it is a larger, low rectangular structure with a sloping transparent roof. The sides of a cold frame are usually made of wood or brick and the roof light is normally in a wooden frame. Some cold frames have transparent sides but this is less common. A cold frame is more permanent than a cloche and often occupies a fixed site. The frame is ventilated, a little or a lot, by sliding the roof or removing it altogether. In extreme weather a cold frame can be covered with old carpets or similar to give extra protection to the plants inside.

Plastic is now being used to replace glass in cold frames. Twin wall polycarbonate is the best material as it is shatterproof and a good insulator. Some structures, made of slightly opaque corrugated plastic, are being marketed as cold frames. Many of these are small and would be better described as cloches.

Uses

A cold frame is a boon to a polytunnel or greenhouse owner as a means of hardening off plants. Plants in trays or pots are transferred directly from the polytunnel to a cold frame. This removes the tiresome business of carrying plants out in the morning and returning them at night. Once in the cold frame, the plants are subjected to increased ventilation until

A cold frame made from polycarbonate and aluminium angle

the top is left off the frame both day and night. This process takes 2 to 3 weeks and varies according to plant type and weather conditions.

In summer cold frames are used for half hardy crops such as ridge cucumbers. In winter cold frames are used to protect hardwood cuttings and seeds of hardy woody subjects such as trees. They are also used in the same way as already described for cloches, except that the plant is taken to the frame whereas the cloche is carried to the plant.

Chapter Two

Propagation & Growing

PLANT CARE IN A POLYTUNNEL

The domestic polytunnel differs from a greenhouse in that a polytunnel is large enough (and cheap enough) to grow a much larger range of plants in raised soil beds. The polytunnel also gives the protection necessary for the plant propagation and crop production usually associated with greenhouses.

Signs that the compost in a plant pot, or tray may be dry:

- The leaves appear slightly dull.
- The surface of the compost looks dry.
- The compost is shrinking from the edge of the pot.
- The pot, or tray, feels lighter than an obviously wet one.
- The plant is wilting.
- If the pot is clay, a tap with the knuckles produces a high ring.

Signs that the compost in a plant pot, or tray may be too wet:

- A polytunnel plant may also be too wet and this may cause the death of a plant.
- The surface of the compost looks wet.
- The surface of the compost appears sealed with no apparent air passages.
- The pot or tray feels heavy compared with a normal one.
- The plant is wilting.
- If the pot is clay, tapping with the knuckles produces a dull thud.

Watering The Polytunnel

The success of the polytunnel gardener depends upon his or her skill at watering. Most polytunnel plants should not be watered until there are signs of dryness. The skill is to recognise a plant's need for water well before it wilts.

Either rain water or mains water can be used for polytunnel watering. Mains water can be used straight from the tap, or from a previously filled tub that is kept inside the polytunnel. The water in the tub is often a little warmer than straight from

Watering Tips At A Glance

- A fine rose should be used for seeds and seedlings.
- Large plants in pots are watered without a rose, the water is applied directly but gently to the surface of the compost.
- After watering wet the polytunnel paths; this is called 'damping down'.

the tap, but this advantage is probably outweighed by the presence of algae and the possibility of bacterial and fungal contamination. If a tub is used it should be kept covered and cleaned regularly. A few potassium permanganate crystals (just enough to lightly colour the water) added to the water helps to keep it disease free.

A Haws type watering can is the most suitable for a polytunnel; it is well balanced and the long spout makes reaching plants at the back of the staging an easy matter.

An attempt to dry out an over-watered geranium

Haws watering cans, the best type for cloches and polytunnels

plant out of its pot and stand it on several sheets of dry newspaper. Return the plant to its pot a few days later.

It is so easy to give more water to plants in the centre of the bench than those at the front and back; it is a good idea to check the effectiveness of your watering now and again:

• Water the plants in your normal way.
• Half an hour later take two pot plants from the back of the bench, two from the middle and two from the front.
• Knock the plants from their pots and examine the rootballs for moisture.
• Replace pots and return the plants to the bench.
• During winter, plants use much less water than they do in summer but they do need a little. Over-watering is very likely to occur in winter, checking moisture levels with a moisture meter helps to avoid the problem.
• The compost in a very dry growbag can be difficult to wet; a little washing-up liquid added to the water may help.

• Damping down is not necessary in winter, nor on cold, humid autumn days.
• Damping down helps to reduce the temperature on very hot days.

A pot plant that has been over-watered is difficult to dry out. One method that sometimes works, is to tap the

A water meter measures the level of water in the compost. This is a valuable aid to good watering, especially in winter

The Use Of Capillary Matting

Capillary matting is a felt-like material that soaks up and holds water. If a waterproof level bench is covered with capillary matting and one end is immersed in a tank of water the matting will remain wet. If the tank is kept filled with a

Capillary matting and micropore plastic

ball valve or a 'glug' bottle, the matting on the bench will be permanently wet.

Standing plant pots and trays on permanently wet capillary matting removes the need for watering. To prevent plants from rooting into the matting, a cover of micropore plastic is placed over the matting before the plants are positioned. Micropore plastic also eliminates the problem of algal growth on the matting. Micropore plastic and capillary matting are available from garden centres or by post from Simply Controls (☎ 01264 334805). Module trays, designed to produce plant plugs, are very difficult to water; standing a tray on a piece of capillary matting removes the problem.

A capillary bed on a polytunnel bench. A piece of rain water gutter is fixed along the front edge to hold water. the capillary matting, covered with micropore plastic, dips into the gutter

Problems With Capillary Matting

Problem	Solution
Some plants need to dry out between waterings e.g. pelargoniums and succulents	Do not use a capillary bench for these plants
As there is no drainage, fertilisers may build up to harmful levels in the compost	Water from the top once a week to correct this
Algae grows on the surface of the matting	Cover with micropore polythene
Roots grow from the bottom of pots into the matting. When moved the roots are broken and the plant checked	Cover matting with micropore polythene. This material does not impare capillary action and it reduces evaporation
Clay pots have a single hole and do not take water from the bed	Make a wick from a strip of capillary matting and thread it through the hole
A capillary bed makes plants too wet in winter	Do not use in winter
Plants become too wet in summer	Remove plants for a few days

Details of a capillary bed.

- micro-perforated polythene
- capillary matting
- plastic sheet
- polystyrene
- marine plywood

water

An odd piece of down-spout over a stake is an effective way to prevent the hosepipe from damaging plants

The Use Of A Hosepipe

A no-return valve must be fitted to the tap.

During the summer months, it is possible to make use of a hosepipe for some of the watering. Extreme care must be taken not to wash compost from the pots or to splash soil on the foliage and fruit as 'soil splash' is a major cause of disease. Ideally the hosepipe should be fitted with a rose and the water pressure kept fairly low.

Seep Hoses

Seep hoses are available in garden centres or by post from Parallax (☎ 0115 9663836).

A seep hose is a hosepipe with very small perforations along its length. It is laid flat on a soil bed or threaded through a growbag and connected to a water supply. Water gradually seeps from the hose to maintain water levels. The amount of time the seep hose needs to be turned on varies with the weather, the stage of crop growth and the water pressure. A shallow tray, placed level under a length of the hose, gives a guide to the amount of water delivered. When using a seep hose, check the soil moisture level with a moisture meter to make sure that your plants are getting enough water and none is being wasted.

Overhead sprayline – not recommended in a domestic polytunnel

Overhead Spraylines

Overhead spraylines are used in many commercial polytunnels where a single crop is grown. They are not suitable for the domestic polytunnel as pots and trays are not watered effectively and the weight of water may cause foliage on some bed-grown plants to collapse.

Composts

A soil which supports perfectly good plants in the polytunnel bed is quite useless when used in growbags, plant pots or trays. The material used in plant pots is called 'compost' and is different from the compost made in a compost heap. Throughout this book the word compost refers to the compost of the plant pot unless otherwise specified. There are good and 'not so good' soils – there are also good and 'not so good' composts; this should be borne in mind if tempted to purchase a cheap bag of compost or a cheap growbag. Some composts contain soil and some do not.

Soil Composts

These were researched many years ago by the John Innes research institute and are therefore called John Innes composts (J.I.). John Innes composts do not store well as some chemicals in them break down to form ammonia which is harmful to plants. They can however be made at home and used when freshly made.

The Ingredients

Loam. This is produced by stacking turf upside down, covering it with black plastic to prevent weed growth and leaving it for a year. (Good riddled topsoil is a viable alternative to loam). The loam should be sterilised to destroy weed seeds, soil pests and fungus diseases.

Peat. Granulated sphagnum moss peat is the most suitable. Leaf mould is a possible alternative to peat, this is made by stacking a cubic metre of autumn leaves in a surround of chicken wire. Decay to mould takes from 10 to 20 months, depending upon the type of leaves collected.

Sand. The sand must be coarse with no fine material. On no account should brick-layers' sand be used, it is too fine; nor sand from the beach, it is too salty. Sand can be replaced with perlite or vermiculite which are easily obtainable and are very much lighter.

Chalk or slaked lime. A small quantity may be needed to reduce the acidity of the loam. Test with a pH meter or litmus test (from garden centres). Add lime if the pH is less than 6.0.

John Innes base. This provides the compost with the essential plant nutrients and is a mixture of:

Hoof & Horn	– two parts
Superphosphate	– two parts
Potassium sulphate	– one part

John Innes base is available ready mixed and there are also alternatives such as Vitax. There are two types of John Innes composts, one for sowing seeds and one for growing plants. The plant compost is numbered 1, 2 or 3 according to the amount of nutrient it contains. Compost should be mixed with a clean spade on a clean concrete floor. John Innes seed compost is made by mixing together:

2 parts loam
1 part peat
1 part coarse sand (or substitute)
1 gram per litre superphosphate

John Innes potting compost is made by mixing together:
7 parts loam
3 parts peat
2 parts coarse sand (or substitute)

To this mixture is added:

for Number 1 compost 3 grams per litre of J.I. base (for pricking out delicate seedlings)
for Number 2 compost 6 grams per litre of J.I. base (for the majority of pricking out and potting up)
for Number 3 compost 9 grams per litre of J.I. base (for plants that make rapid growth, e.g. tomatoes)

All parts by volume. A two gallon bucket holds around 10 litres and makes a useful measure.

If large quantities are to be made it may be worthwhile making a measuring box with the internal dimensions of 50cm (20in) long, 20cm (8in)wide and 10 cm (4in)deep. When level full this box holds exactly 10 litres.

Soil Free Composts

John Innes composts are heavy to handle and their main ingredient, good loam, is not easy to obtain. John Innes composts are better used freshly made as they deteriorate in store. For these reasons John Innes composts have been largely replaced by no-soil composts.

Research has produced some excellent peat-only composts which, in addition to growing good plants, are light in weight, odourless and pleasant to handle. These composts have been so successful that peat extraction is now threatening whole ecosystems.

The main alternatives to peat are bark and wastes from the coconut and chocolate industries. There is now a wide range of soil free composts both with and without peat. Virtually all soil free composts give good results, providing the grower is aware of the small differences in growing and watering techniques described elsewhere in this book.

Home-Made Soil Free Compost

Soil free composts can be made at home with a certain amount of cost saving. There is no need to sterilise any of the ingredients but mixing should be carried out on a clean floor. Sphagnum moss peat gives best results. The peat should be slightly dampened and spread on the floor to a depth of around 15cm (6in). The fertilisers are sprinkled as evenly as possible over the surface and then the compost is thoroughly mixed with a clean spade.

Ingredients for home-made compost:

Sphagnum moss peat	100 litres
ammonium nitrate	40g
superphosphate	150g
potassium nitrate	70g
magnesium lime	300g
ground limestone	300g
fritted trace elements	35g

The fritted trace elements are obtainable from Garden Direct (☎ 01992 441888) or Vitax (☎ 01530 510060). These companies also sell ready mixed fertilisers for no soil composts. A ready mixed base is recommended as, in addition to being much easier, a single weighing is likely to be more accurate than six individual ones.

Note: some heathers, azaleas and other plants thrive only in acidic soil conditions. If these are being grown the magnesium lime and ground limestone must each be reduced to 50g. An acid compost is known as Ericaceous and can be purchased from garden shops and garden centres.

Peat Free Composts

Environmental concern about the use of peat by growers and gardeners has led to the introduction of a number of peat free composts. The author has tested six of these and compared them with the best peat composts available.

The Composts Tested:

Bio Peat Free Multi-purpose
Made from coconut fibre, loam and sand. Judging by the light weight it is mostly coir with a small proportion of loam and sand.

Goldengrow Multi-purpose
A very fine compost made from the coir element of coconut husks. It claims to 'need less water than peat'. I don't know what is meant by this, it is the plant that uses the water – not the compost.

Levington Peat Free Universal
Stated on the bag: 'Made from recyclable materials of U.K. origin'. Probably another way of saying 'Made from bark and/or wood'. A rather coarse compost that is nice and 'open'.

New Horizon Peat Free
It says on the bag that it is made from 'a renewable resource of U.K. origin' with added vermiculite and perlite.

Shamrock Peat Free Multi-purpose
Made from composted bark. Somewhat finer than the Levington peat free one.

Shoots Organic Growing Medium
Coir with no added fertilisers. Dairy waste and other natural materials supply the nutrients.

Levington Multi-purpose
Peat based.

J A Bowers Multi-purpose
Peat based.

John Innes No 2
Peat based.

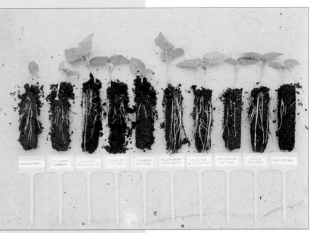

Runner bean plants in root trainers – part of a compost trial

Compost trial – dahlias

Conclusions from the trial:
- All the composts performed well.
- The peat based composts were slightly better than the peat free ones.
- The John Innes compost was the least successful.
- Composts based on bark were less likely to 'slump' than composts based on coir. (Shoots compost was the exception – it did not slump).
- Coir composts are finer and therefore better for sowing very small seeds than the bark based ones.
- Bark based composts were a little easier to water than the coir based ones.

Compost trial – busy Lizzies

Bark compost – no slumping *Peat compost – little slumping* *Coir compost – badly slumped. The composts had been in the tubs for 6 months*

The author's recommendation to gardeners who wish to change from a peat compost to a peat free compost:

- Find a local supplier of one of the composts on the list above (they are all good).
- Buy a bag and use it alongside the peat compost. Take extra care with watering.
- When the new compost is proving successful, stick to that one and stop buying peat.

Gardeners who tried out coir compost several years ago, did not like it and returned to peat, should try again – the new generation of peat free composts are now very much better.

Glossary Of Words That Refer To Composts

Loam: *sterilised rotted turfs – a humus rich soil with fairly equal parts of sand, silt and clay.*

Coir: *the outer husks of coconut. A coconut has a thick outer case that consists of a mass of tough fibres.*

Vermiculite: *made from mica, a mineral that is mined in South Africa. When heated to a very high temperature it expands to expose lots of surfaces, all of which hold water. Vermiculite is less stable than perlite and breaks down in its second year. When buying vermiculite, care should be taken to get the horticultural grade. Industrial vermiculite is alkaline and may have been treated with a water repellant.*

Perlite: *made from a type of volcanic rock. After crushing, the rock is heated and expands like sugar puffs. Perlite holds lots of air and keeps a compost 'open'.*

Sand: *sand used for bricklaying is no use for compost. Compost sand must be coarse and clean with particles between 1.5 – 3mm diameter. Sand helps a compost to drain and increases the amount of air.*

Multi-purpose compost: *a compost that can be used for sowing, potting and for cuttings.*

Potting compost: *a compost that should only be used for potting and pricking out. This compost is unsuitable for seeds as the fertiliser it contains may damage the shoot as it emerges from the seed.*

Seed compost: *suitable for sowing seeds but unlikely to have sufficient nutrients for pots or containers.*

Seed compost is usually only available in small bags, this makes the price per litre rather expensive. To make it go further, two thirds fill your containers with multi-purpose compost and then top up with seed compost. If the seeds need covering use vermiculite. The seeds will germinate in seed compost and soon have their roots in multi-purpose compost, where more nutrients are available.

Plant Containers

Standard pots, trays, half trays, divided trays and modules of the types normally used in greenhouses are also suitable for use in a polytunnel. In addition root trainers are very useful and superior to pots and trays for raising some types of plants.

Mixing in perlite to make compost more suitable for cuttings

Pots

Plastic pots are cheap, easy to clean and are available in square shapes as well as round. Square pots have the advantage of fitting together and so using all the available bench space. This is an advantage when plants are small but as the plants grow pots are moved apart to prevent leaves from touching and to give sufficient light and air. When used for sowing seeds, more square pots will fit into a propagator than similar sized round pots. House plants are better in round pots as most jardinieres are designed for round pots. The size of a pot refers to the top diameter, this means that there are several sizes of 13cm (5in) pots as they have different depths. The British pot is

Trays used in the polytunnel

deeper than the continental one and 'pans' are shallow in comparison. Pans are used for germinating seeds. The standard plant tray is 35cmx21cm (14inx 8in) and this is useful when fifty or so of one type of plant is wanted, where fewer plants are needed a half tray should be used. Some half trays are available divided into sections of six or nine. These are very useful for larger plants and high value plants such as geraniums. Trays vary in depth, the shallower ones are for seeds and the deeper ones for pricking out.

A half tray divided into modules

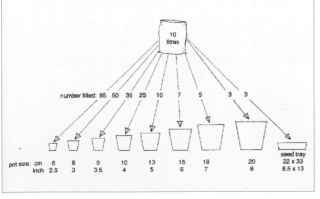

The number of pots which 10 litres of compost will fill. Use this information to decide how much compost to buy

Root Trainers

Root trainers were developed in Canada for growing trees. They are now manufactured in this country and are almost essential in the polytunnel. A trainer is a single piece of plastic that folds in half to form a number of long, thin cells. Each cell is intended to hold one plant. The cells have fluted sides which direct roots downwards, as the tip of the root grows out of the bottom it dries up and dies. This encourages the side roots to grow and a brilliant root system forms – a plant is only as good as its roots! That is not all. The trainers open and close like a book which allows inspection or transplanting without root damage. Ten trainers are held in

41

Root trainers

StoneWool

An alternative to sowing in a compost is to use StoneWool cubes. These are completely sterile and are recommended with high value seeds. Sow one seed in each cube and keep well watered in a propagator. When roots appear at the edge of the cube, plant the whole thing in a pot of multi-purpose compost. StoneWool does not contain any fertilisers so transferring to compost should not be delayed. Cubes are available from Growth Technology (☎ 01823 325291) which also supplies special fertilisers for hydroponics (growing plants without soil or compost).

Tray of StoneWool cubes

a frame which occupies roughly the same space on the bench as a standard seed tray. Ten trainers hold either forty or fifty plants depending upon the size of the cells.

Root trainers are easy to clean and they are good value for money as they can be used over and over again. In the polytunnel root trainers have the following uses:

- **Germinating seeds:** beans – broad, French and runner. Peas and sweet peas, sweetcorn, cabbage, cauliflower, leeks and many more.
- **Pricking out:** tiny seedlings which are intended for hanging baskets such as lobelia and begonias. The long, tapered root system makes inserting into the side of a hanging basket very easy.
- **Cuttings:** root trainers allow a lot of cuttings in a small space. Cuttings are placed in alternate cells leaving other cells empty.
- **Filling Root Trainers:** to fill a block of root trainers, pile compost over the top and work it towards the out sides. Consolidate the compost by lifting the trainers a couple of inches and dropping them. Pile more compost over the top and work it into the half-empty cells. Use a plant pot as a scoop to fill the corner cells and finally brush any surplus compost from the top.

Jiffy7s

A Jiffy7 is a disc of compressed peat/coir mix surrounded by a degradable plastic net. When soaked the Jiffy7 expands into an extremely useful plant growing cell.

Filling the corner cells with the aid of a plant pot

Brushing surplus compost from freshly filled trainers

Jiffy7s are widely used in commercial horticulture and are available to amateur gardeners from garden centres or by mail order from Johnsons (freephone: ☎ 0800 614323). Jiffy7s can be used for sowing seeds (one per Jiffy) pricking out and for cuttings. They provide an excellent rooting environment and are planted up (net and all) with no root disturbance. Any gardener who has difficulty in rooting cuttings should give Jiffy7s a try.

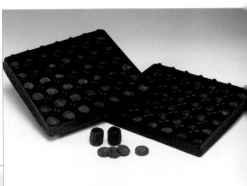

Jiffy7s in trays as supplied by mail order. The six loose in front show the difference between unexpanded and expanded ones

Sowing Seeds

One of the easiest and best methods of propagating plants is from seed. A seed consists of a protective coat covering a tiny plant and a food store. When given water, air and warmth the tiny plant is nourished by the food store and begins to grow. This process is called 'germination'. Most seeds will germinate in darkness but some require light.

Seeds are sown in either seed compost or multi-purpose compost; if potting compost is used there is a danger that the fertilisers present will damage the seeds during the first stages of germination. It is most important that containers are correctly filled, it is false economy to save compost by only half filling them.

If the seeds are large enough to handle, place them evenly in a standard seed tray in five rows of eight, this will save the need to prick out later. If the seeds are small, tip them on to a piece of strong white paper. Hold the paper above the compost and dislodge the seeds by gently tapping the

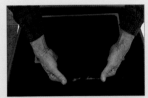

Pile compost over the tray

Check that the corners are filled

Use a board to level off

Firm gently

Water with a rose can

edge of the paper. Distribute the seeds evenly over the compost. Do not sow too thickly or the seedlings will become tall and spindly and are much more likely to damp off. A 9cm (3½ in) square plant pot is an ideal size for small seeds and when pricked out will fill two or three standard trays. Most seeds require covering, the larger the seed the deeper the cover required. Large seeds such as peas and beans are covered with a layer of compost. Compost is not ideal for covering smaller seeds as it sometimes forms a mat that is lifted by the germinating seeds. Then the seedlings are useless and spindly from lack of light. Horticultural grade vermiculite is the best material to cover seeds, it is very light and almost transparent. Small seeds need only a light cover, just enough so they cannot be seen. Very small seeds like begonia or lobelia should not be covered, a smart tap on the side of the pot will shake them into the compost.

Sowing broad bean seeds in root trainers. Each seed is pushed down to the same depth

What is meant by thinly sown? The mustard seeds are thickly, normally and thinly sown. Note that in all three pots the seeds are evenly sown

The uneven growth and development of these geranium plants shows the effect of sowing at different depths

Covering seeds with vermiculite

Label the seeds with the variety and the sowing date. Place the tray or pot into a propagator and adjust the thermostat (for most seeds 18°C - 24°C [65°F - 75°F]).

If the seeds are to be germinated on the polytunnel bench, slide the tray into a large polythene bag and leave the end open. Place the label upright in the centre of the tray to keep the plastic above the compost. Shade from direct sunlight with a sheet of newspaper.

Nearly all seeds will germinate at lower temperatures than stated here but they will take longer and the risk of failure will increase. Some seeds (e.g. hardy primulas and butterhead lettuce) will not germinate at high temperatures and should be placed in a cool part of the polytunnel or left outside with some protection.

Inspect at least once a day and as soon as the seedlings can be seen, remove the tray from the bag or propagator. Prick out the seedlings as soon as possible and certainly before the first true leaf appears.

Primed Seed

Some seed suppliers offer 'primed seed'. These seeds have been brought to the point of germination and remain in that state. Primed seeds germinate more quickly and more evenly than unprimed seeds, especially at temperatures which are lower than ideal. Seedlings from unprimed seeds soon catch up and after a few weeks there is no obvious difference. Gardeners who have difficulty in germinating some types of seeds may find the extra cost of primed seeds worthwhile.

Runner bean seedlings in root trainers

Pricking Out Seedlings

Seedlings, produced by the method just described, do not have enough space to develop. They soon become tall, spindly and quite useless as plants. Each seedling must be given space to grow, this is done by digging them up and replanting them individually in pots or spaced out in seed trays. Transplanting seedlings into pots is called 'potting up'. Transplanting seedlings into trays is called 'pricking out'. Seedlings should be pricked out as soon as they are large enough to handle.

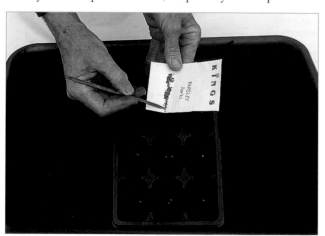

Sowing in divided trays

Propagators manufactured from expanded polystyrene are very energy efficient

Seedlings ready for pricking out

Lower the seedling to the correct depth

Gently firm the compost round the stem

Pricking Out Seedlings:

- Fill a plant tray almost to the top with potting compost or multi-purpose compost.
- Gently firm the compost and water with a rose can. The compost should be damp but not waterlogged. (A good test is to take a handful of the watered compost and squeeze it. Water should appear between your fingers but not drip onto the floor).
- Write a label. Include the date the seeds were sown.
- On the compost mark the position of the plants in the top row and the left hand side row. Eight rows of four plants and ten rows of five plants are common populations for a standard seed tray. The beginner should aim for the lower number.
- Take a small dibber (no larger than a pencil) and gently dig up a clump of seedlings.
- From this clump tease out a single seedling, holding it carefully by a leaf. A seedling should never be held by the stem – it can grow a new leaf but not a new stem!
- Using the dibber make a hole in the compost at the top left-hand corner of the tray.
- Insert the seedling. If the root is too long for the hole allow it to curl round until the plant is the correct depth – see diagram.

- Gently firm the compost around it – like putting a baby to bed!
- Complete the top row, then complete each row in turn. Care must be taken to put only one seedling at each station – even with small plants such as lobelia and begonia. Where seedlings are very small the standard practice is to prick them out in small clumps but I find that individual seedlings produce better results.
- Place the tray of seedlings on the staging in good light, but avoid direct sunlight for a few days.

Potting Up

Seedlings are not potted up into their final pots straight away, they are moved from small pots into larger pots as they develop.

There are two reasons for this:

1. Small pots take less space, making better use of the polytunnel bench.
2. A plant grown in this way has a better root system than one that started life in its final pot. When potting up seedlings with a soil based compost fill the pot 5mm ($^1/_4$in) below the rim of the pot. When using a soil free compost fill the pot almost to the brim – this will help to prevent over-watering.

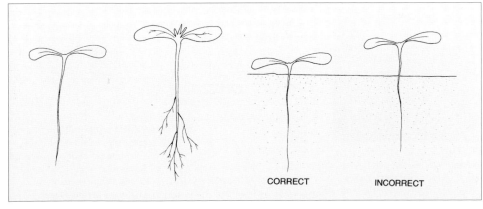

CORRECT   INCORRECT

A seedling should be pricked out when it is in-between these two stages of development.
The correct depth at which to prick out a seedling.

45

Potting On

Transferring a pot-plant into a larger pot is known as 'potting on'. The larger pot should be either one size or at the most two sizes bigger than the pot the plant is in.

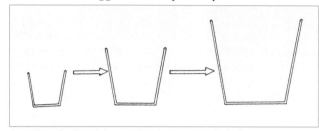

As a plant develops it is potted up into progressively larger pots

- Water the plants which are to be potted on and leave to stand for half an hour.
- Put a layer of compost into the bottom of the larger pot and place the plant, pot and all, onto it. Add or remove compost until the brims of the two pots are level.
- Knock out the plant from its pot as shown opposite. If roots are coiling around the bottom, gently tease them out.

Removing a plant from its pot. If slight pressure on the corners does not release the root ball from the pot, tap the top edge of the upside-down pot on the edge of the bench

- Place the plant centrally in the new pot.
- Fill the space around the sides with new compost and gently firm it. Do not apply any pressure to the old root ball, or the roots may be damaged.

Note: Some soil free composts require very light compaction. Water with care and place on the staging to grow.

Firming the compost during potting on. To avoid root damage the thumbs should always be in contact with the edge of the pot

Cuttings

If part of a plant is removed and kept in the right conditions, the cut may develop a callus from which roots grow. This results in a new plant. Plants raised by this method will have exactly the same characteristics as the parent plant. The part which is taken from the parent plant is called a cutting.

There are different types of cutting, some plants propagate easily from a stem cutting, whilst others are best propagated from a leaf or bud.

A polytunnel is an excellent place to propagate from cuttings and even better if a little 'bottom' heat is available in the form of a propagator. A cutting is most likely to succeed if:

- the temperature is suitable for plant growth.
- there is a good supply of air to the base of the cutting.
- water is available at the cut end.
- the atmosphere around the leaves is humid.
- bacteria and fungi that cause disease are absent.
- auxins (hormones) are present at the cut.
- there is good light – but not direct sunlight.

Rooting Medium

The substance in which a cutting is placed to form roots is called a 'rooting medium'. This medium must have lots of air spaces, hold water and have no disease organisms. It must have only a very small amount of nitrogen fertiliser present or none at all. Once cuttings have formed roots they will require a supply of nitrogen. This can be given as a light feed or by using a container with rooting medium at the top and potting compost at the bottom.

There are many different kinds of rooting mediums. One of the most successful which can be made at home is:

Equal parts of fine grade Cambark and medium grade sphagnum moss peat, mixed together.

Almost as good is:

Equal parts of a multi-purpose compost and perlite mixed together.

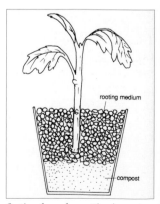

Section through a cutting in a pot. The rooting medium is supplying air and water to the base of the stem. When the roots reach the compost they will obtain the nutrients necessary for healthy growth

Either of these rooting mediums can be used for the cuttings which are described on the next few pages. Treasured cuttings, and those from expensive plants, are best rooted in Jiffy7s or StoneWool cubes (page 42).

Rooting Powder And Rooting Gel

Rooting powder or rooting gel (obtainable from all garden shops and centres) contain a plant hormone which aids success as it speeds up rooting.

A little rooting powder in the lid to dip the cuttings. If the container is used the powder may become wet and spoil.

The cut end is coated in powder by dipping in and shaking off the surplus. The cutting should not be dipped into the container as the powder may become wet and spoil. A very small quantity tipped into the lid is ideal for dipping and any surplus can be discarded.

Stem Cuttings

There are three types of stem cuttings, young stems (softwood), middle-aged stems (semi-hardwood) and old stems (hardwood). In practice softwood cuttings are new growth taken in spring, semi-hardwood cuttings are new growth taken in summer and hardwood cuttings are new growth taken in autumn. Softwood cuttings root quickly and hardwood cuttings root slowly, with semi-hardwood somewhere in between. A semi-hardwood cutting should bend through ninety degrees with one finger without breaking.

Propagating By Soft Wood Cuttings

• Select a container which is well drained and at least 10cm (4in) deep. A 12cm (5in) pot will take five cuttings. Root trainers will take up to fifty but it is better to put a cutting in every other cell which means 25 cuttings per block.

• Fill the container with rooting medium and firm this by lifting the container a couple of centimetres (an inch) or so and dropping it onto the bench. Do not press the medium down as this reduces the amount of air.

• Water with a rose can and leave to drain.

• Select young vigorous shoots near to the base of the plant rejecting any with flower buds. Cut off around 10cm (4in) of each shoot and place them in a polythene bag. Some plants, marguerites for example, often have a flower bud at the end of every shoot. Take the cutting and remove the flower bud.

Dahlia and chrysanthemum cuttings ready for taking

• Prepare each cutting by removing the bottom of the stem with a clean square cut just below a node (leaf joint). Remove any leaves and buds from the bottom half of the cutting, leaving two or three (but no more) at the top. If the lowest leaf is large, remove half of it.

• Make a hole in the medium with a small dibber, dip the lower end of the cutting into rooting powder and insert it leaving 1cm ($\frac{1}{2}$in) of clear stem above the medium. Fill the hole with medium and firm very gently. Repeat with the other cuttings until the container is filled.

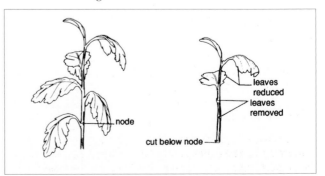

An unprepared and a prepared cutting

- Place the container of cuttings into a heated propagator with the lid on. If a propagator is not being used arrange a transparent plastic cover with a frame of split canes to hold the plastic away from the cuttings.
- After a couple of weeks test for signs of rooting. This is done by gently pulling a cutting, if you feel a little resistance it means that roots are growing.
- As soon as the cuttings have rooted open the polythene bag by slitting it across the top, do not remove it as sudden removal may cause the cuttings to collapse. Three or four days later remove the bag.
- Pot up the cuttings in small pots. Place them on the

Cutting covered with a polythene bag

polytunnel staging until ready for potting on or hardening off.

Ten Hints For Success With Softwood Cuttings

1. Take cuttings from strong vigorous growth – either from a young plant or from the new growth of an old plant that has been recently cut hard back.
2. Use a very sharp knife – and keep it sharp.
3. Use material completely free from pests and diseases.
4. Use vegetative shoots i.e. no flower buds.
5. Insert the cutting as soon as it has been prepared, except for pelargoniums.
6. Collect cutting material in a polythene bag as this reduces water loss.
7. Remove any soft tips that wilt.
8. Use a hormone rooting powder to speed up rooting.
9. Do not push the cutting directly into the medium – make a hole with a dibber.
10. Ensure that the leaves are not resting directly on the surface.

> **Species which propagate easily from soft-wood cuttings in a polytunnel:**
> Begonia; Bidens; Dahlia; Carnation (perpetual flowering); Chrysanthemum; Coleus; Fuchsia; Geranium (pelargonium); Solanum; Plumbago; Passiflora; Plectranthus; Surfinia.

Propogating By Semi-Hardwood Cuttings

- Select the current year's side growths which are soft at the top and hard at the bottom.
- Pull them away from the stem in such a way that a small piece of old stem is attached. This is called a 'heel'.

Problems With Cuttings

Problem	Cause	Solution
Cuttings turn black at the base and die	Shortage of air in the medium	Use a more open medium – add more grit or perlite. Take care not to get the medium too wet
The leaves become mouldy	Fungus disease, botrytis	Use sterilised medium. Make sure that the container is clean
Cuttings appear healthy but fail to root	Low temperature, or slow rooting species	21°C (70°F) is best for most cuttings. Some species take longer than others

- Remove the bottom leaves, take out any old wood at the base of the cutting but leave the bark.
- Trim off any straggly bits of bark.
- Immerse the whole cutting in a weak fungicide for a few seconds.
- Treat in a similar way to that described for soft wood cuttings.

Hundreds of species can be propagated by softwood or semi-hardwood cuttings, including many of the popular hardy shrubs. It is a good idea to go around the garden in June and take softwood cuttings from all available shrubs and attempt to root them in the way described above. Repeat the exercise 5 or 6 weeks later and try semi-hardwood cuttings from the same species.

Propagation From Hardwood Cuttings

- During November collect 20-25 cm (8-10 in) lengths of the current year's growth.
- Cut off the top immature part, just above a bud, making a sloping cut which leaves the bud near to the top.
- Make a square cut at the lower end, just below a bud. Remove all the buds except for the top three. With black currants and other plants which are grown as a stool, leave all the buds on.
- Fill 12cm (5in) Full pots (Continental pots are not deep enough) with rooting medium level to the top.
- Make five holes in the medium with a dibber and dip the lower end of each cutting into rooting powder.
- Immerse the cuttings in a weak fungicide for a few seconds.
- Insert the cuttings to a depth which leaves the lowest bud 2cm (1in) above the top of the medium. The base of the cuttings must be well clear of the bottom of the pot – if this is not so, shorten them.
- Keep in the polytunnel throughout the winter with the compost slightly moist but not wet. Do not allow the compost to freeze solid – plunge the pots into a soil bed to prevent this.
- Successful cuttings will begin to grow in spring, pot these up and grow-on in the usual way.
- An alternative method is to make 20cm (8in) slits in a soil bed, trickle some grit into the bottom of the slit to a depth of 5cm (2in). Place the cuttings on the grit and fill the slits with soil.

Hardwood Cuttings

Fruit trees, roses and many garden shrubs (both evergreen and deciduous) are easily propagated from hardwood cuttings. A polytunnel is ideal for hardwood cuttings.

Propagation Of Conifers

- One-third fill small pots with potting or multi-purpose compost. Fill to the top with perlite, vermiculite or very coarse sand.
- Water well and cover the top with cling film, secure this with selotape or a rubber band.
- Use secateurs to cut off lengths of new growth including about 3cm (1in) of brown wood.
- Clear the bottom 5cm (2in) of stem by snatching off the side growths. This wounds the brown part of the stem and aids root formation.
- Moisten the wounded end and dip it into rooting powder.
- Make a small hole in the centre of the cling film and insert the cutting so that the end is in the centre of the pot i.e. in the rooting medium and 1cm ($^1/_2$in) or so above the potting compost.
- Place on the polytunnel bench and shade from direct sunlight. Some frost will not harm the cuttings but do not allow the pots to freeze solid or the new roots will be destroyed.

The cuttings will have rooted by spring, pot them up into 8cm (3in) pots. Grow on in the polytunnel for a few weeks before hardening off for use outside.

Conifer Cuttings

Most conifers are easily propagated from cuttings. A polytunnel is ideal for this purpose as the cuttings are taken in October when the summer crops have finished.

Feeding Plants In The Polytunnel

Plants use about sixteen different elements to build their tissues. Some are used in large amounts and some in very small amounts – micro nutrients or 'trace elements'. If one element is in short supply growth and development will suffer. Most well managed soils will contain all the necessary chemicals for good, healthy plant growth – but not maximum plant growth. Adding nitrogen to the soil will usually increase the yield. Shortages of nutrients are corrected by adding chemical fertilisers to the soil or compost. Gardeners call this 'feeding'. In the polytunnel, plants in pots and trays are usually fed each week during the growing season.

Element	Part Most Affected	Signs Of Shortage	Effect Of Adding Too Much
Nitrate	Leaves	Yellow colour of leaves	Rank, spindly growth, delayed maturity
Phosphate	Roots	Poor growth, blue colour on leaves	Effects not easily seen
Potash	Flowers and fruit	Leaf margins die	New growth small and tinted with blue

Plants in soil beds obtain most of their nutrients from the soil. One dressing of fertiliser is normally sufficient for these. The exceptions are tomatoes and cucumbers that benefit from a weekly feed even when they have their roots in the soil.

The three elements that are most often in short supply are nitrogen (nitrate), phosphorous (phosphate) and potassium (potash). These elements affect the plant in different ways as illustrated in the chart above.

A complete fertiliser will state the proportions of nitrogen, phosphate and potash it contains.

These proportions are given as single numbers: 10:5:8 means 10% nitrate, 5% phosphate and 8% potash. In addition to the three main plant foods, good fertiliser will contain the full range of trace elements. The small print on fertiliser packets often uses chemical shorthand, N = nitrate, p = Phosphate and K = potash. The numbers on fertiliser containers are always put in this order: nitrate first, phosphate second and potash last.

Badly fed plants are more likely to suffer from pests and diseases than well-fed ones.

The plant on the left has not been fed. The one on the right had a weekly feed of Phostrogen

Feeding Polytunnel Plants

- Select two complete fertilisers from the large range that is available in garden shops. One that is high in nitrogen (e.g. 20:10:10) and one that is high in potash (e.g. 15:15:30). Make sure that your selection has trace elements. It is preferable to buy a fertiliser with the trace elements listed in the contents than one that just says 'added trace elements'.
- Begin feeding in early spring as growth commences and feed as routine on a certain day each week. Use the high nitrogen feed.

- Add the feed to the normal watering strictly in accordance with the manufacturer's instructions. Do not overfeed and do not feed wilting plants – water them, and feed the following day.
- When fruit and flowers begin to appear, change over to the high potash feed (an ideal time for tomatoes is when the first truss is fully set).

The Thru Hose Feeder

Liquid, Powder, Granules and Tablets

Fertilisers are available in a number of different formulations. Liquid fertilisers used to be easier to dilute than powdered ones. Most powders (or crystals) are now so soluble that there is little difference in ease of use. Granules are intended for spreading evenly over the soil; they are easier to handle than powders. Tablets contain slow release fertilisers, that is they supply nutrients over a long period of time. Tablets are expensive but useful in containers and hanging baskets.

Foliar Feeding

Plants will absorb small amounts of nutrients through their leaves, wetting the leaves as well as the soil may replace a deficient element a little more quickly. Roots are the major nutrient absorbing organs and it is usually better to apply plant feeds directly to the soil or compost. Note: plants should not be foliar fed in direct sunshine.

Automatic Feeding

Time saving systems are available for feeding plants in a polytunnel. The Phostrogen Thru Hose Feeder is one that works extremely well. There is no measuring to be done and feeding takes the same time as the normal watering. This feeder, with its container of fertiliser, is connected to a tap; the hose is connected to the feeder and the water becomes a weak liquid feed. The strength of the feed is altered by

turning a dial on the feeder. A Thru Hose Feeder, permanently fixed near to a tap, is a real boon. Just set the dial, turn on the tap, and water the plants directly with a hose. When feeding small pot plants, fill a watering can with the hose and the water will contain the correct amount of fertiliser.

The Thru Hose Feeder has six settings, four of which are used in the polytunnel. The settings mean:

Setting	Application when used with **Phostrogen plant food**
5	Mature plants with a high fertiliser requirement, e.g. tomatoes & chrysanthemums
4	Cabbage, other vegetables and plants in pots size $22^1/_2$cm (9in) and over
3	Plants in smaller pots, trays of seedlings
2	This setting is for lawns and a different fertiliser
1	Special applications beyond the scope of this book
0	Water only – use this setting 6 days a week

The plant that gets most water gets most fertiliser. If the plants receive a normal watering on the day they are fed the amount of fertiliser they receive will be about right. Regular feeding is essential; it is a good idea to feed all the plants on the same day each week.

Chapter Three

Flowers

Marguerites – stock plants for cuttings always in flower in the polytunnel

Non-stop begonias are good pot or border plants. These were grown in the polytunnel from purchased plugs

The polytunnel can be used to grow flowers for cutting, flowering plants for the house and conservatory, hardy plants for the garden and annuals for the borders.

Bedding Plants

Gardens that are a mass of colour in spring are often rather disappointing at the height of summer. Bedding plants grown in the polytunnel will fill borders with summer colour that lasts until the first frosts of winter. Seed catalogues have almost 500 different bedding plants on offer, some of which have a fairly short flowering season. The twelve listed right are ideal for raising in a polytunnel and will flower over a long period.

An excellent, but uncommon bedding plant is sanvitalia – also called creeping zinnia. A group of these at the front of a border, is quickly covered with miniature 'sunflowers' and spreads onto the path. Cleome (spider flower) is a good choice for the back of a border – or a single ricinus (caster oil plant), 1m (3ft) tall and standing proud. The flowers are not striking – but the large bronzed leaves are real head turners and a constant joy from June until October.

Sow in March or early April. Take great care with nicotiana as the seeds are very small – unlike the seeds of ricinus which are large and need to be sown, one seed per pot, at a depth of $2\frac{1}{2}$cm (1in). Take special care if children are around – ricinus seeds are as poisonous as they are attractive.

Bedding Plants To Give A Bright Summer Border

- African Marigold Inca Gold
- Alyssum Snow Crystals
- Cleome Mixed
- French Marigold Safari Bolero
- Nicotiana Domino Salmon Pink
- Petunia Carpet Series Mixed
- Phlox Tapestry
- Ricinus Impala
- Rudbeckia Indian Summer
- Salpiglossis Carnival
- Sanvitalia Procumbens
- Tagetes Tangerine Gem

This annual border was in flower from mid-June until October. The plants were all purchased by post as small plugs or seedlings. These were received on the 2nd of April, potted up and grown on in a polytunnel until the end of May. They had no heat but were covered at night when frost was forecast. They were hardened off during the last week of May and the first week of June before being planted out

All should be germinated in a heated propagator and transferred to the staging as soon as they begin to germinate. If you do not have a propagator germinate them in the house instead. Seeds will germinate on the staging in a polytunnel but they take much longer and germination is less reliable.

As the seeds germinate, prick out seedlings into trays (except cleome which are best pricked out individually in 9cm [3½in] pots) and transfer them to the polytunnel staging. Whenever there is a danger of frost, cover with one or two layers of fleece at night.

All the flowers, except African marigolds, will be in flower from the end of June until late September. African marigolds start flowering about 3 weeks later but they are well worth waiting for!

Do not sow too early, later sowings tend to catch up whilst seeds sown very early make slow progress and may become drawn and rootbound.

There are of course many other bedding plants that can be raised in a polytunnel – the ones listed are the author's favourites. Tender subjects such as salvia splendens and impatiens (busy Lizzie) are less likely to succeed. The more difficult bedding plants can be grown quite easily in a polytunnel by purchasing plant plugs – small plants growing in modules – potting them up and growing on for 6 weeks or so until the weather is suitable for hardening them off.

Biennials & Perennials

After the bedding plants have been moved outside, the space on the bench can be used for raising biennial and perennial plants to flower the following and subsequent years.

Prick the seedlings out into divided trays or individual pots and grow them on the bench. At the end of summer, harden them off and plant into the flowering positions.

Black eyed Suzy is easy to grow from seed. Use as a house plant or grow it outside on trellis where it will succeed in a warm sunny place

Some of the perennials listed will flower in the first year if sown very early
Canterbury Bell
Carnation
Chrysanthemum (Korean hybrids)
Coreopsis
Bellis (Daisy)
Delphinium
Dianthus
Forget-me-not
Foxglove
Gaillardia
Lewisia (sow February, prefers cold – do not use a propagator)
Lupin
Pansy
Polyanthus
Primula
Viola

Ranuculus corms planted in pots in the autumn (claws down) make excellent cut flowers in early spring. The plants are hardy but do not allow the pots to freeze

Planting A Hanging Basket

- Obtain the largest suitable basket.
- Stand the basket on a 22cm (9in) pot.
- Line the bottom half of the basket with moss or woolmoss (a moss substitute made from scrap wool).
- Cut a circle of plastic, half the diameter of the basket, and place it in the bottom to form a well.
- Half fill the basket with a good multipurpose compost (not John Innes as it is too heavy).
- Place the recommended number of *osmocote (or other slow release fertiliser) tablets on the top.
- Plant up a number of trailing plants by feeding the plants through the side and putting the roots into the compost. If the plant is too large for the hole in the basket, roll paper around it to form a tube before feeding it through.
- If the basket is to be hung against a wall, leave one side unplanted.

Grow prepared hyacinth bulbs individually in pots. When they reach this stage they can be planted into bowls. Select those at the same stage of development in order to have them flowering all at the same time

Polyanthus flowering in January from seeds sown in June

- Line the top half of the basket.
- Add a little more compost.
- Take the larger, pot grown plants, remove the pots and arrange them on the compost with the soil level about 1cm ($\frac{1}{2}$ in) below the top of the basket.
- Fill the spaces between the pots with compost, firming it gently to avoid leaving any empty space.
- Plant a few more trailing plants around the edge, allowing them to overhang the side.
- Cover the surface of the compost with moss or woolmoss.

- Water well.
- Hang the completed basket in the polytunnel. If frost is forecast cover the basket with fleece. Water daily until the weather conditions are suitable and hang it outside. Take the basket inside for the first few nights to harden the plants off.
* Osmocote tablets contain a slow release fertiliser and remove the need to feed.

Note: Hanging baskets use a lot of water and need daily attention. They even need watering on rainy days. The best way to check if a basket needs watering is to test its weight by lifting from underneath.

Hanging Baskets

The polytunnel is an excellent place for hanging basket production and to raise the flowers that fill them. In the first year of polytunnel ownership it may be necessary to purchase stock plants. These plants will fill the first year's baskets and then provide cuttings for later years. Hayloft Plants (℡ 01386 561235) offer a good selection of excellent plants by post.

Perennial hanging basket plants are raised by taking cuttings in March from plants that were themselves raised from cuttings taken the previous August and over-wintered in the polytunnel.

Annual hanging basket plants are raised from seeds in a similar way to bedding plants.

The secret of a good hanging basket is to have the largest one possible. Small ones are more difficult to maintain than large ones as they dry out very quickly. Moisture retaining agents are available for mixing with hanging basket composts (e.g. Chempak supergel). These increase the water capacity but they make no difference to the amount of water the plants use.

The same baskets one month later in their summer positions

Select strong growing shoots with a healthy, active growing point. Carefully snap off any flowers or flower buds

Snap off the lower leaves. Each cutting must have at least one leaf joint

Hanging Basket Plants Which Can Be Grown From Seeds In A Polytunnel:	
Plant	Sowing Date
Alyssum	March
Brachycome	April
Campanula fragilis	March
Marigold	March
Nasturtium	March
Nolana	March
Petunia	March
Sanvitalia	March
Tagetes	March

Cut the stem just below the leaf joint using a clean sharp knife

Finally, tear off the green leaf-like stipules attached to the leaf joint. If left on they may rot and infect the cutting with a disease

Raising Hanging Basket Plants

Cuttings of trailing half hardy perennials are best taken from the baskets in August or early September. Surfinia petunias will probably survive the winter in the polytunnel, providing they are given some extra protection during very cold weather. Other basket plants such as Helichrysum petiolare and Plectranthus australus (Swedish ivy) are more tender and will need a little heat to survive the coldest part of winter. This last sentence will not apply to all areas of the U.K. Heat can be provided by a propagator, set the thermostat at 5°C 41°F and close the top at night. In February increase the amount of water and, when there are signs of growth, give a half strength tomato feed each week. In March take cuttings from the new plants and strike them in Jiffy7s in a propagator with some bottom heat. When rooted the cuttings (Jiffy7 and all) can be potted up in 9cm (3¹/₂ in) pots. Place these on the polytunnel bench (adding protection during frost) and they will be an ideal size when required in

May. Dozens of plants can be propagated from the two or three that were overwintered in the propagator. The value of these plants should far outweigh the cost of any electricity used.

Take geranium cuttings in August, allow them to dry for 24 hours before inserting in the rooting medium. Pot up individually and water very sparingly until early October. Stand the pots on a soil bed, covered with a sheet of plastic, such as 'Terratex' and cover with several layers of fleece. Do not water them during the winter. In March, place the pots on the bench and treat in a similar way to the cuttings described above.

Tuberous rooted begonias are widely used in hanging baskets. At the end of the season, lift the tubers from the basket, brush off the compost and allow the plant to die down. Dust the tubers with a little sulphur and pack them in dry peat, and store in a cool frost proof place. In February transfer them to a warm room.

Inspect the tubers regularly and when shoots begin to appear, pot up in a soil free multipurpose compost, shoots uppermost and cover with 2cm (1in) of compost. Grow on in the propagator and transfer to the staging when conditions are warm enough.

Trailing lobelia is an excellent hanging basket plant. The seeds are extremely small and it requires a long growing season. Seeds, sown in early February will produce suitable plants by May. Germinate them in a propagator and prick out into small root trainers. The long, narrow root balls feed easily through hanging basket wires.

Border and pond edge plants which may not be hardy in a bad winter can be saved by lifting, potting up and transferring to the polytunnel. This lobelia cardinalis and penstemon are examples

Note: It is often possible to purchase geranium, lobelia (trailing) and begonia (fibrous rooted) seedlings from garden centres for little more than the cost of the seeds.

Flowers For Cutting

The polytunnel can be used to produce masses of cut flowers including the following:

Antirrhinum (not bedding type, use F1 variety for greenhouse cut flowers. Sow early July for flowers in December).

Brompton stock (plant out after sweetcorn for spring flowers).

Chrysanthemum (in pots – plunged into beds after tomatoes are finished).

Gomphrena (excellent everlasting flower– many flowers from a few plants).

Gypsophila (for bunching with sweet peas),daffodil and other spring bulbs (bulbs planted in soil beds in the autumn flower earlier than those outside).

Sweet pea (early crop from autumn sowing and spring planting).

Sweet William (raise from seed, plant out after tomatoes – flowers in spring).

Brompton Stocks

Brompton stocks are brilliant, they have cheerful colours and superb scent. They are excellent cut flowers which fill the gap between the spring bulbs and summer blooms. Brompton stocks make good use of polytunnel staging after the bedding plants have gone and even better use of soil beds or growbags after the tomatoes have finished. Best of all – no heat is required!

Antirrhinums sown in July make good cut flowers in early December

Growing Brompton Stocks

- Sow seeds in pans or trays in May.
- Prick out into trays and grow on.
- When the plants fill the trays pot them up into 12½ cm (5in) pots filled with multi-purpose compost.
- Grow on in a polytunnel. Feed weekly with Miracle-Gro, Phostrogen or Sangral.
- In November, when the tomato (or other crop) is finished, plant Brompton stocks in their place 30cm (12in) apart.
- Water sparingly – the soil not the leaves.
- Give plenty of ventilation and if any grey mould appears spray with a systemic fungicide.
- In spring increase watering and give just one liquid feed.
- Cut the flowers as soon as they are ready. The side shoots will produce a second crop.
- When flowering has finished, clear the area and prepare for your regular summer crop.

Brompton stocks in flower in April. They produce a large crop of excellent cut flowers. It is not possible to select all doubles – the singles have as much scent

Sweet peas in root trainers in November almost ready for stopping

Sweet Peas

Sweet peas are an excellent polytunnel crop for early cut flowers. They are quite hardy and easy to grow. They produce a large crop of long stemmed, fragrant flowers from a small area of soil.

Make two sowings of sweet peas, one in November for flowering inside and a second in January to produce plants for flowering outside. Some books recommend sowing sweet peas in September, with these early sowings the plants are in a hopeless tangle before the soil is warm enough for planting. Also recommended is the removal of part of the seed coat with a knife, this is difficult and quite unnecessary – if the method opposite is used.

Sweet peas in May; excellent scented flowers with long stems

Growing Sweet Peas To Flower In A Polytunnel

- Fill large root trainers with multi-purpose compost and wet it thoroughly.
- Sow one seed in each section about 2cm (1in) deep.
- Place in a heated propagator and leave it there until the first seeds are emerging.
- Transfer the root trainers to the polytunnel bench and leave to grow – a slow process.
- When the plants have three leaves, pinch out the tops. This is most important as the resulting side shoots are stronger and more vigorous than the main stem.
- In February/March, plant out in a well-manured soil bed in a double row. Space the plants 15cm (6in) apart and the rows 30cm (12in) apart.
- Fix a vertical net, as high as the polytunnel will allow, for the plants to scramble up.
- Keep well watered, and pick the blooms regularly – do not leave any to form pods.
- When the blooms become short stemmed (and short lived) pull up the plants and replace with a summer crop.
  An alternative way is to use the cordon method:
- Remove all, but two, of the side shoots from each plant.
- After planting out push in the tallest possible garden cane for each stem i.e. two per plant.
- Remove all tendrils and sideshoots as they appear.
- Fix each stem to its own cane with sweet pea rings.
- Harvest all flowers as soon as ready.
- When a stem reaches the roof, remove the rings, lay it on the floor and allow the tip to grow up again.
  The cordon method is time consuming but the quality of the flowers is better. The plants crop over a longer period – which may not be desirable in a polytunnel.

Gypsophila Elegans

This annual plant is traditionally added to bunches of sweet peas. It is quite difficult to time the sowing of gypsophila so that the flowers are ready at the same time as the sweet peas. Sow thinly in pots in February and germinate in a propagator. Grow on until the roots are holding the soil ball together. Make pot-size holes in the corner of a soil bed. Remove the pots and, taking great care not to disturb the soil balls, 'sit' the seedlings in the holes. Gently firm and water. Apart from watering and weed control, no further attention is needed until the crop is ready for cutting.

Other Cut Flowers From Seed

Many hardy annuals can be grown in a polytunnel for cutting (or display) 4 weeks or so earlier than outside crops. One of the most successful is larkspur which can be raised in root trainers and planted outside (after being thoroughly hardened off) or planted in the polytunnel for even earlier flowering.

Flowers such as gomphrena (an excellent 'everlasting' flower as it keeps its colour after drying) will produce many flowers from a very small area. Any odd space that becomes available during the summer can be very usefully filled with a few of these.

Chrysanthemums make good use of the polytunnel after the summer crops have finished

Chrysanthemums

Chrysanthemums can be very successful in a polytunnel. They survive some frost and are out of the way during the summer when the polytunnel is filled with tomatoes, cucumbers and other tender crops. In autumn and early winter they produce attractive and valuable cut flowers.

Shorter varieties can be grown in tubs or pots and moved into the conservatory for flowering during November and December.

There are several different shapes of chrysanthemum flowers and many different colours. The important difference as far as the grower is concerned, is between 'spray' chrysanthemums – a group of small flowers at the head of a long stem and 'bloom' chrysanthemums – a large individual flower at the head of a long stem. Apart from disbudding, 'sprays' and 'blooms' are grown in the same way. Varieties which are advertised as 'sprays' must be grown as sprays as they will not make good 'blooms'. Similarly 'bloom' varieties do not make good sprays.

The flowering time of a variety of chrysanthemum is governed by the length of the night. The varieties that will flower from late September to late November are most suitable for a polytunnel as they follow crops such as cucumber, melon and sweetcorn. Later flowering varieties require some heat to lower the humidity and prevent fungus diseases. Although the mature plants will withstand frost, the flowers will not; the plants must therefore be covered with fleece at night whenever frost is forecast. A recent practice is to transfer late flowerers from the polytunnel to the conservatory to give colourful flowers until the New Year.

Growing Chrysanthemums In The Polytunnel For Cut Flowers

Use a small watering can to thoroughly moisten the roots with tepid water. Take care not to mix-up the labels before potting

Getting Started

- Consult specialist catalogues such as Elm House Nursery (☎ 01945 581511). Select October and November flowering varieties and order rooted cuttings which will arrive in the spring.
- Pot up the cuttings in 9cm (3½in) pots filled with a good potting compost. Do not firm the compost.
- Place on the polytunnel staging and water the compost. Do not water again until the compost is almost dry. After the second watering, keep the compost moist but not wet.
- When the plant has six full sized leaves, pinch out the top. This is known as 'stopping'.

Stopping induces the lower buds to 'break' (grow) and several flowering shoots form instead of just one. Sometimes a plant will produce premature flower buds (these are much larger than the buds on the other plants). Any plant with this type of bud, should have half its stem removed.

- When the roots fill the compost, pot on into a 13cm (5in) pot.
- Feed regularly with a liquid plant food (see the recipe on page 64).
- As the weather begins to warm, harden off and transfer the plants outside.

Fill a 9cm(3½in) pot with multi-purpose compost and make a hole in the centre, just big enough to take the young plant's rootball

Pot-up, keeping the plant upright, making sure that the top of the module of compost is level with the compost in the pot

Add a little more compost to fill the pot. Level off the top with your thumbs but do not press the compost down at all

Slide the label between the pot and the compost. Water thoroughly – do not water again until the compost has almost dried out

Unprepared and prepared chrysanthemum cutting

Spider chrysanthemums, the flower arrangers' delight - are as easy to grow in a polytunnel as any other type of chrysanthemum

Dwarf chrysanthemums are grown in tubs in the polytunnel and transferred to the conservatory for flowering. This tub was in flower for 6 weeks

Chrysanthemum cuttings in individual 9cm (3¹/₂in) pots. These plants will soon be ready for potting on

Outside Work

- Pot up into 23cm (9in) pots. There is no need to purchase expensive compost, a home made John Innes number 3 potting will be cheaper (see page 38). Firm the compost hard around the outside edges of the pot, using a short length of wood the thickness of a broom handle. Keep the wood against the edge of the pot or the root ball may be damaged.
- Stake each plant with a 1.4m (4ft) cane in the centre of the pot and tie each stem to it. Or stake with four canes around the edge of the pot and tie strings around the canes to encircle the plant. Staking is most important otherwise the stems break away at the base.
- Mark the top of the cane to indicate which are bloom varieties and which are spray varieties. The author uses a little blue electricians' tape around the canes on the blooms. This avoids mistakes when disbudding.

- Place the pots in a line on a hard surface. To prevent pots from blowing over, tie the tops of the canes to a horizontal wire stretched between two posts.
- Water as required. Feed each week with a tomato fertiliser, diluted according to the manufacturer's instructions.
- A home-made feed is a little cheaper:
    150g (5oz) of potassium nitrate
    60g (2oz) of ammonium nitrate
- Dissolve in 1 litre (1.75 pints) of water. Dilute the solution 300 times, that is 3ml in 1 litre (1fl.oz. in 15 pints) and water the chrysanthemums with it once a week.

Disbudding

For blooms:
As the sideshoots develop break them off. Leave the small buds at the top of the stem to develop. When the top group of buds are large enough to handle, remove all of them except the terminal bud – this will become the flower. The purpose of this is to produce one large flower with a long stem.

For sprays:
When the terminal bud is large enough to handle, remove it. The purpose of this is to have a group of flowers, open at the same time, on a single stem.

Flowering

- The actual timing of the move into the greenhouse will vary according to district. The aim is to avoid any frost on the flower buds. Carry the plants into the polytunnel pot first. Line them up leaving 45cm (18in) either way between the pots.
- Give maximum ventilation, only closing at night when frost is forecast.
- Continue to water and feed.
- Cut the blooms complete with a long stem. A flower is ready for cutting when the outside petals are spread and the inside ones still in a cluster.
- Remove the leaves from the bottom half of the stem.
- Crush the bottom 3cm (1in) of the stem with a hammer or pliers.
- Stand the flowers in a bucket of water overnight. The water should almost (but not quite) reach the blooms. This 'conditioning' increases the vase-life of the flowers.
- When all the flowers have been cut, discard any plants that show signs of weakness or disease.

Preserving The Stock

- Select one or two of the better stools of each variety.
- Cut off any regrowth and place them in a sheltered position outside the polytunnel.
- Leave the plants outside until there has been a week's cold weather when temperatures have not risen above 5°C (40°F). Frost at this stage does more good than harm.
- After this treatment remove all the dead leaves and return the plants to the polytunnel. During periods of intense cold it may be necessary to give some protection to prevent the compost in the pots from freezing solid. Plunging them into a soil bed will usually suffice.
- In late February give a little water.
- As spring sunshine increases temperatures and new shoots appear, increase the watering but do not feed.
- When the shoots are large enough, take cuttings (see page 46), in most districts this will be during April.
- Discard the stools.

Note: The stock may become diseased as years go by. To avoid this, purchase new cuttings every third or fourth year.

Chrysanthemums spend summer outside and flower in the polytunnel during October and November

Chapter Four

Fruit

Two growbags provide an ideal rooting space for a cucumber plant

A polytunnel is an ideal place to grow half hardy and other fruit, including:

Aubergines	Peppers
Cucumbers	Strawberries (forced in pots)
Grapes	
Melons	Tomatoes

Aubergines

The new F1 varieties of aubergines crop well and make a worthwhile polytunnel crop (try Money-maker – it is excellent). If you have not grown aubergines before try two or three plants and look up a good moussaka recipe!

Aubergines are grown in the same way as peppers with one or two important exceptions:

- Seeds must be sown in February or early March as a longer growing season is needed.
- Somewhat cooler conditions are required in summer for the fruit to set; positioning near to a door will probably ensure setting.

- Aubergines must be harvested whilst the skins are still shiny. Fruit that has become dull is rather tough and unappetising.
- Any fruit that hangs on the soil should be protected by slipping a board underneath.
- Plants may require a single stake to stop them from falling but no training is needed, just let the plants do their own thing.

Aubergines – the board is to protect the fruit from the soil

to eat. The aim of the gardener is to produce fruit from unpollinated flowers; this can be achieved in two ways:

- Removing all the male flowers before they open.
- Growing a variety of cucumbers that has no male flowers – just female.

The second method is strongly recommended.

Cucumbers grow very quickly but they require a warmer environment than tomatoes; for this reason sowing should be delayed until the cherry trees are in full blossom. If the first lot of plants fail due to cold weather there is plenty of time to repeat. With this in mind, sow only half the seeds at a time. Cucumber plants are easy to grow; they are also easy to kill. Regular care and attention to detail will avoid the latter.

Cucumbers

Cucumbers can be satisfactorily grown in the same polytunnel as tomatoes; the common belief that this is not so should be ignored. A well-grown cucumber plant will produce up to fifty full sized cucumbers during the growing season.

The cucumber plant produces both male and female flowers. Unlike other species the cucumber produces fruit from unpollinated as well as pollinated flowers. Fruit from pollinated flowers is bitter and not very nice

Growing Cucumbers

Cucumber plants are readily available from garden centres. It is much better to raise your own as you are then certain that they have not been chilled in transit.

Raising The Plants

A StoneWool cube gives a cucumber seedling a good start

- Select an F1 hybrid variety that produces only female flowers. There are many to choose from. Both Fenumex and Birgit perform well in a polytunnel. If your garden is in a cold area try Crystal Lemon – the fruits are small, round and pale but they are a good flavour and produced in abundance.
- Use clean 15cm (6in) pots and one third fill with a sterilised, free draining seed compost. The small amount of compost needed can easily be sterilised in a microwave oven. Put it into a plastic roasting bag and 'cook' on high for one minute.
- Hold one seed between finger and thumb and push it into the centre of the pot to a depth of 1cm ($^1/_2$in).
- Water the pots and place them in a propagator set at 25°C (75°F) or the highest setting if it is lower than this.
- After germination, which takes 2 or 3 days, leave the plants in the propagator. Make sure that there is some ventilation and the propagator cover is as clean as possible to admit maximum light.
- When the seedling reaches the top of the pot, add extra compost up to within 1cm ($^1/_2$in) of the seed leaves.
- Feed the plants each week with half strength tomato fertiliser.
- When daytime temperatures are above 21°C (70°F), remove the plants from the propagator and place them on a bench in the lightest part of the polytunnel. At night cover them with a piece of horticultural fleece.

Planting

- Cucumbers will grow well in a soil bed, providing the soil has warmed up before planting. An alternative to a soil bed is to use two growbags, one on top of the other. Cut a large hole on the top of the bottom bag and a corresponding hole on the bottom of the top bag. The cucumber will root into both bags and produce many more cucumbers than it would in a single growbag.
- When the plants have enough roots to hold the root-ball intact (but before the roots circle the bottom of the pot), water well. Carefully knock each plant out of its pot and plant it with the minimum of root disturbance. Leave the surface of the root-ball 4 or 5 centimetres (a couple of inches) higher than the soil or compost. This prevents a pool of water from collecting around the stem and reduces the risk of stem-rot.
- Water carefully and thoroughly.
- For the next few days, isolate the plants from the rest of the polytunnel with a sheet of polythene to maintain a humid atmosphere around them. If the nights are likely to be cold (below 10°C / 50°F) cover with fleece.

Crystal Apple, an easy to grow and heavy cropping cucumber

Training

- Tie strings or wires across the area where cucumbers are to be grown. Horizontal wires should be 25cm (9in) apart.
- Tie the main stem loosely and vertically to one of the supporting strings.
- Remove all the sideshoots and flowers from the bottom 20cm (8in) of the main stem. This will help to prevent the fruit from resting on the ground and becoming soiled or possibly diseased.
- As new sideshoots appear tie them along the horizontal strings.
- When there is one sideshoot growing along each support, remove all other sideshoots as they appear – including sideshoots on sideshoots.

Ridge cucumbers are easier to grow than most greenhouse varieties

Note: If a variety that produces male flowers is grown, the training is a little different. With these varieties the fruits are produced on the sideshoots and not the leaf joints. Pinch the sideshoots off one leaf beyond each developing fruit.

Harvest

- Do not delay harvesting as this will reduce the yield.
- A cucumber is ready to harvest when its lower end is becoming rounded.
- Hold the cucumber in one hand and cut through the fruit's stalk with the other.
- Remove the harvested fruit from the polytunnel immediately and wrap it in a single layer of cling film. Store in a cool room – not in the refrigerator.

Grapes

A long polytunnel is not an ideal place for a vine due to the possibility of fungus disease in the autumn. Short polytunnels often have better ventilation and good crops of grapes can be grown.

A grape vine grows very rapidly – controlling rank summer growth and thinning bunches of grapes is very time consuming. If time is short this crop is best left to others.

Growing Grapes

- Mark out an area of slightly more than 1m (1yd) square inside the polytunnel.
- Dig out the soil to a depth of at least 60cm (2ft), pile up the topsoil and discard any subsoil that is brought to the surface.
- Place a layer of brick rubble in the bottom and cover this with a layer of inverted turfs.
- To the pile of topsoil add:
- 5x10 litre (2gal) buckets of well-made organic waste compost or well-rotted farmyard manure.
- 300g ($\frac{1}{2}$lb) of ground limestone.
- 100g (3oz) bone meal.
- a spadeful of woodash.
- Mix the topsoil and return it to the hole.
- Obtain a container grown vine of a variety that is suitable for a polytunnel. Black Hamburg or Fosters Seedling (white) is suitable but new ones are being developed which may be better.
- Dig a hole larger, but not deeper than the container.
- Remove the container, tease out the roots and spread them in the bottom of the hole. Fill in the hole, making sure that the vine is not planted any deeper than it was in the container.
- Tread to firm the soil and water well.
- If the vine is dormant, cut back to 1m (1yd) after planting. If the vine is a young growing one, cut right back leaving just two buds. As these develop train the better one as a leader and cut the other one off.
- Decide where the vine is to grow and fix wires accordingly. If the main stem is to be taken along the roof it should be on the north side to keep shading on other plants to a minimum.
- As the leader grows tie it along the wire.
- Laterals (side growths) will appear, these should either be trained at right angles to the main stem or removed.

- Nip off all the non-fruiting laterals after the seventh leaf. Nip out the tips of the fruiting laterals, leaving two leaves between the fruit and the end.
- Water regularly. Vines need large amounts of water and must not be allowed to dry out.
- After flowering give a liquid feed each week with half strength tomato fertiliser.
- Aim for one bunch of grapes per 20cm (8in) of stem. Cut out all the other bunches.
- When the grapes are about the size of small peas, thin out the individual bunches. Use a pair of fine pointed scissors and, working from the bottom, snip out small clusters of grapes leaving individual grapes with about 1cm ($\frac{1}{2}$ in) between them. Failure to do this will result in useless tiny fruit and a lot of fungus disease.

Note: Special grape scissors are obtainable.

- Throughout the summer the vine will produce more sideshoots and flowers. Rub these out as they arise.
- Harvest the grapes as they ripen by cutting off whole bunches with secateurs.
- Reduce watering.
- When the plant is dormant cut back the main rod (stem) to leave about 1m (1yd). Any laterals that remain on this should be cut back to two buds.
- Rub the old wood hard with a gloved hand to remove loose bark.
- Remove all dead leaves and prunings.
- When growth begins the following spring, sprinkle 100g (3oz) of complete fertiliser around the base and apply a thick mulch to the soil.

A vine restricted to one corner of a polytunnel. This plant needed pinching back all summer but it did produce fifteen good bunches of grapes

Melons

The introduction of F1 varieties of melons (e.g. Sweetheart) has made growing them in polytunnels worthwhile with up to ten fruits per plant. The fruits are smaller than imported melons but the flavour is excellent. The best time to sow is when the cherry blossom is dropping its petals. Melon is a suitable crop to follow sweetpeas, carrots or early potatoes.

Growing Melons

- Fill 9cm (3½in) pots with multi-purpose compost, and sow seeds individually by holding in between the finger and thumb and pushing them 1cm (½in) deep.
- Germinate in a propagator at 21°C (70°F) and grow the young plants in good light on the staging.
- If the plant becomes too large before the previous crop is harvested, pot it up to a larger pot.
- When space is available, transplant into a soil bed that has been well manured with rotted farm yard manure or well-made organic waste compost (growbags may be used instead – one plant per bag).
- Arrange strings, net or trellis on which to train the plants.
- Water regularly but avoid getting the soil too wet.
- Tie the leading shoots upwards (there is often more than one). When they are about 1m (1yd) long, pinch out the tops.
- Train side shoots either horizontally or in a fan.

- Melons produce lots of male flowers and few female ones. The first flowers are usually males, do not worry the females will appear – one on each sideshoot. Pinch out the growing point one leaf beyond each female flower.
- Make sure that there is a strong, loose tie either side of the female flower. This will support the fruit and there will be no need for the sling that is often recommended.

An excellent variety of melon – Sweetheart

- During bright sunshine remove a fully open male flower, take off its petals and transfer pollen to the female by touching the flower centres together.
- Remove a second male flower, take off its petals, place it inside the female flower and leave it there. If no insecticides are used there should be enough insects around to make this hand pollination unnecessary.

A water melon. The plant produced one large melon which proved very difficult to ripen

- When the fruits begin to change colour, reduce watering and give plenty of ventilation. This is necessary as a fungus control measure.
- Test for ripeness by taking the fruit in your hand and applying a little gentle pressure to the blossom end. If the fruit gives a little it is ready for harvest.
- Cut through the stalk with a sharp knife and keep the melon in a warm room to complete ripening.
- After all the fruit has been gathered, remove the plants and place them on the compost heap.

Melon flowers – male flower on left, female on right

Peppers

Peppers are an ideal crop to grow in a soil bed after peas, spinach or early potatoes have been harvested. Peppers can also be grown in a growbag – three plants per bag.

When well grown in a polytunnel, sweet peppers produce a very worthwhile crop. Unlike cucumbers and tomatoes, peppers freeze well and a temporary glut is therefore not a problem. Green peppers, like green tomatoes, are unripe red or yellow ones. Peppers are slow to ripen and larger crops will be obtained if the fruit is harvested whilst still green.

Pepper plants thrive in similar conditions to those of tomatoes, so the two crops can be grown in the same polytunnel.

Peppers grow exceptionally well in a soil bed

Growing Peppers

- Sow seeds in late March or early April and germinate in a propagator set at 18°C (65°F).
- Prick the seedlings out into 10cm (4in) pots of multi-purpose compost and place on staging.
- If frost is forecast, cover the plants at night with horticultural fleece.
- When roots are filling the pot, transplant to either a soil bed 40cm (15in) apart or growbags (two plants per bag).
- Support each plant with a single cane and a string tie.
- Keep a sharp lookout for aphids.
- Water regularly and feed each week with a liquid tomato fertiliser.
- Harvest the fruit as soon as they are a reasonable size, by cutting through the stalk with a sharp knife.

Strawberries

Strawberries can be produced at least 4 weeks earlier in a polytunnel than outside. As strawberry plants age they lose their vigour. It is essential therefore to obtain plants, either by propagating from a young healthy bed or by purchasing certified plants in the autumn. The variety Gorella is probably the best for a polytunnel but any early variety can be used.

Growing Early Strawberries

- In early July fill 15cm (6in) pots with potting compost and partially sink them alongside the best plants in a strawberry bed. Peg the first young plant on a runner onto the compost and nip the tip of the runner off to prevent it from growing further. A length of string threaded through the bottom of the plant pot and brought up through the compost is better than a peg for securing the runner.
- When the young plants have rooted into the pots, detach them from the parent plants or pot up purchased plants.
- Plunge the pots into a bed of sand or coal ashes. During August and September keep the plants growing with a weekly feed of liquid fertiliser.
- Leave the plants outside until late January. This is very important as a period of cold is essential for bud formation.
- At the end of January, take the plants into the greenhouse and either arrange them on the staging or transplant them into a growbag (six plants per bag).
- Water as required – but not too much!
- When the first flower buds can be seen, begin a weekly feeding routine with a low strength liquid fertiliser.
- As the weather becomes warmer, increase daytime ventilation.
- Brush the open flowers with cotton wool or a rabbit's tail. The flowers are self fertile, brushing helps move pollen from the male to the female parts of the flower.
- Pick the fruit as it ripens.
- After fruiting, discard the plants as they will not force successfully the following year.

Tomatoes

The polytunnel provides an excellent environment for growing tomatoes. Very large crops can be obtained from a single plant. In the Midlands polytunnel grown tomatoes are regularly harvested from the end of June until early November. Sixteen trusses per plant is quite common. In the autumn ventilation is more important than temperature. If unheated polytunnels are left closed on damp autumn days grey mould becomes a severe problem.

Planting in a soil bed is an easy and effective method of growing tomatoes

Sizes of popular varieties of tomatoes compared

Varieties

There are many varieties (over 3,000!) with various fruit shapes, sizes and colours. Those with very large fruit are most suitable for cooking, whilst those with very small fruit are said to have the sweetest flavour. The seeds of F1 Hybrids are more expensive than the other types. They are however very reliable and generally worth the extra money.

Purchasing Plants.

If a propagator is not available, tomato plants should be purchased at the beginning of May (Midlands, earlier in other areas). The best plants are fairly dark green and short jointed. Plants that are standing outside shops should be avoided as they are probably receiving a chill. If a propagator is available, good quality tomato plants are easily raised from seeds.

Raising Tomato Plants In A Polytunnel

- Good light is required – do not begin until late February at the earliest.
- Fill 9cm (3$\frac{1}{2}$in) pots with seed compost, water and allow to drain.
- Sow one seed in the centre of each pot by pushing it to a depth of 6mm ($\frac{1}{4}$in) with a cocktail stick.
- Germinate in a propagator set at 25°C (75°F).
- Following germination, reduce the temperature to 20°C (68°F) and leave the plants in the propagator. In warm weather the propagator top can be removed in the daytime to give extra light.
- As the plants grow, move them apart and do not allow them to touch.
- Begin feeding according to the instructions on the bag of compost and feed each week.
- The amount of plant nutrients in a compost varies according to type.
- As soon as the plants reach the top of the propagator, move them into the lightest part of the polytunnel. In cold weather, cover at night with horticultural fleece.
- Check the roots occasionally by tapping a plant from its pot. When they appear at the surface of the ball, pot on into potting or general purpose compost in 13cm (5in) pots. When potting up, put the plant a little deeper than it was before.
- Grow on. As the plants get bigger move them further apart to prevent the leaves from touching.
- When two or three flowers are fully opened plant up into the fruiting positions.

Note: Extra plants can be obtained by using side shoots as cuttings - they root very quickly.

Tomato Fertiliser

After planting out, fertiliser should be withheld until the first truss of tomatoes has set. That is the yellow parts of the flowers have dropped off leaving pea–sized tomatoes.

Correct feeding will keep tomato plants healthy and double or triple the yield of fruit. Tomato feeds are available as liquid concentrates and soluble powders. Most powders are cheaper to use than liquids and are just as good. It is very important that the manufacturers' instructions are carefully adhered to. For plants which are grown in a soil bed, home-made feed produces good results and is much cheaper than the liquid concentrates.

It is usual to feed tomato plants by watering directly onto the compost. Plants can be foliar fed by watering the diluted feed directly onto the leaves. The amount of nutrients taken in by leaves is very small compared with that taken in by the roots. Never feed a very dry wilting plant. Water it first and leave it to recover before feeding.

Home-Made Tomato Feed

- Pour 5 litres (1gal) of water into a plastic bucket.
- Add 750g (1.5lb) of potassium nitrate and 180g (6oz) of ammonium nitrate.
- Stir until the powders have dissolved.
- Transfer to a plastic bottle, suitably labelled.

To use: Add 5ml (1fl oz) or a teaspoon full of the solution to each 5 litre (1gal) of water and apply this at every watering.

Methods Of Growing Tomatoes In A Polytunnel

The best way for the amateur gardener to grow tomatoes in a polytunnel is to plant them directly into a well-prepared soil bed. If the soil has been deepened by raising the bed, so much the better. Plant deep enough to bury 5-7cm (2-3in) of stem. This will produce additional roots and improve the root system. Plants in a soil bed are unlikely to suffer from water stress, they will have access to a good range of trace elements and will benefit from nutrients supplied by manure breaking down in the soil. However for maximum yields regular feeding is also necessary.

If tomatoes are grown in the same soil each year it is very likely that problems with soil pests and soil borne diseases will eventually occur. Where a polytunnel is used for several different crops some rotation can be practised. It is important to remember that closely related plants have similar pests and diseases – tomatoes are very closely related to potatoes and rotating these crops will be ineffective. Various methods of producing tomatoes have been devised and the ones described in this chapter are all well tried and tested.

Operations Common To All Methods

Training

An untrained plant grows into a low spreading bush which is unsuitable for polytunnel production. It takes up too much room and the space above it is wasted. To overcome this, tomato plants are trained upwards as single stems.

- Identify the sideshoots.
- When a sideshoot is about 5cm (2in) long, hold it between the finger and the thumb and apply a little sidewards pressure. The sideshoot will snap off, leaving the leaf below intact.
- Repeat this operation as necessary throughout the growing season.

Tomato Plant Problems

Symptoms	Probable Cause	Possible Cause
Leaves look dark blue; growth hard	Temperature too low	Plants in a draught
Plants very pale green	Not enough light	Temperature too high
Lower leaves yellow, poor growth	Waterlogged	
Curled leaves with shrivelled edges. Very dark green	Overfeeding	
Plants tall and spindly	Pots too close together	Not enough ventilation

Removing a side shoot

Support

- Tie a length of tomato twine (or nylon string) loosely with a knot that will not slip around the stem, 15cm (6in) or so from soil level.
- Hold the twine above the plant and turn it around the stem once or twice.
- Fix the string to a firm support above the plant.
- As the plant grows, give the string an occasional twist around the stem.
- A bamboo cane pushed hard into the soil near to the stem base is an alternative method of support. The plant is tied to the cane every foot (30cm) or so.

Lowering The Plants

This enables extra trusses to be grown on each plant.

- When tops of plants have reached the plastic, do not pinch them out but untie the supporting string and tie another length on to it. Lower plant, by laying the stem on the floor until the lowest fruit is 15cm (6in) from the ground.
- Tie the string to a new support and allow the plant to continue its upward growth.

Watering

In hot weather large tomato plants can use up to 2 litres (3 pints) of water each day. It is important to keep the compost or soil wet, but not waterlogged.

- Check each day and water as necessary.
- Direct a jet of water directly into the flowers. This is very important as it assists pollination and fruit set.
- In early autumn, when the days are shorter and cooler, water the compost but keep the foliage dry.

Lower Leaves

Lower leaf removal will increase air circulation and helps prevent fungus diseases. Older leaves curl and are no use to the plant.

- When the first fruit is picked, cut off the leaves below the first truss with a sharp knife.
- Continue to remove the leaves progressively from the bottom. Do not take leaves above the ripening trusses.

Ventilation

- Give maximum ventilation throughout the summer but always close up at night, this will help to raise the night temperature. A large day/night temperature difference can cause problems with the fruit.
- When the daytime temperature falls below 17°C (64°F) reduce ventilation.
- On damp autumn days have a door open at each end during the day as a fungus control measure.

Harvesting

- Harvest when the fruit is turning colour but is still firm and not fully ripe.
- Remove each fruit, complete with calyx, by lifting upwards and snapping the stem.
- Take the fruit indoors immediately as hot sun will cause it to lose condition.
- Large fruit not ripened by the end of the season will ripen indoors in good light, but not in direct sunshine. It will ripen more quickly if sealed in a plastic bag with a very ripe banana. Smaller green fruit can be used to make tomato chutney.

Removing Tomato Plants

At the end of the season old tomato plants, together with their roots, should be removed as soon as possible. The discarded material should be properly composted, well away from the polytunnel.

Growing Tomatoes By Different Methods

In A Soil Bed

- As soon as the bed is free from its previous crop, dig into the soil a liberal quantity of well-made organic waste compost or farmyard manure. Dig as deeply as possible without bringing any subsoil to the surface. The compost or manure should be well mixed with the soil and not, as is sometimes recommended, placed in the bottom of a trench.
- Spread ground limestone over the surface at the rate of 300g per sq m (10oz per sq yd)

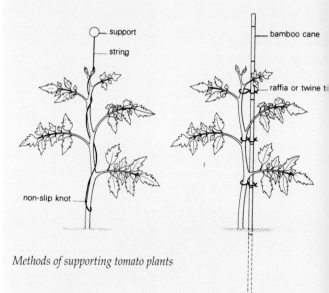

Methods of supporting tomato plants

- Allow the bed to settle for at least 2 weeks (longer if possible).
- Mark out the positions of the tomato plants. Allow a minimum of 40cm (16in) between the plants. If two rows are to be planted they should be a metre (yard) apart.
- Dig a hole large enough to take the root ball and 7$\frac{1}{2}$cm (3in) deeper. Tap the plant from its pot and place it in the hole. Firm the soil around the plant, take care not to disturb the root ball.
- Train and care for as described.
- When the first truss is set (i.e. the petals have fallen and pea-sized fruit is present) begin feeding and continue to do so for the rest of the season.

Growbags

Growbags are a good method of resting soil beds from growing tomatoes. Most manufacturers recommend three plants per bag. As well as less disease and water stress, a better yield is obtained by growing two plants per bag instead of three.

- Purchase good quality growbags.
- Place the bags in their positions on the floor of the polytunnel. Drop a string for each plant from a taught wire above. Tie each string around the bag, leaving a little slack to twist around the plant as it grows.

A better way of using a straw bale, see page 80. The pots have no bottoms and the plants root into the straw. If the bale is kept wet there will be no possibility of blossom end rot

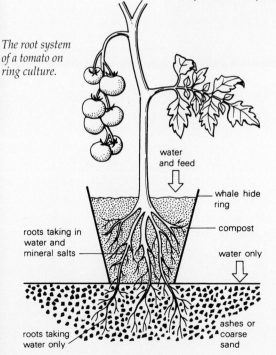

The root system of a tomato on ring culture.

water and feed

whale hide ring

compost

water only

roots taking in water and mineral salts

water only

roots taking water only

ashes or coarse sand

- Cut two holes in the top of the bag, large enough to take each plant.
- Carefully pour 10 litres (2gal) of water into each growbag.
- Make appropriate sized holes in the growing medium by pushing the material sideways.
- Tap the plants from their pots and place one in each hole. Draw the growing medium around the rootball.
- Train and care for as described.
- Begin to feed as soon as the first fruit is set and continue throughout the season.
- A more successful method of growing tomatoes in a growbag is to pot up two plants into $22^{1}/_{2}$cm (9in) plastic pots and grow-on for 2 weeks. Cut two holes in the top of a growbag, the same size as the bottom of the pots. Without disturbing the plants cut the bottoms off the pots and set the bottomless pots on the growbag holes. Cut a smaller third hole between the pots to water the growbag compost. The plants should be fed and watered in the top of the pots and the growbag compost kept moist. The tomatoes soon root into the growbag and will produce large crops.

Ring Culture

- Remove the soil from a soil bed (or use a wooden box), line with plastic and cut drainage holes.
- Fill the hole (or box) with coarse sand, coal ashes or other non-toxic, free draining material.
- On the top of the sand place bottomless 22^1/$_2$cm (9in) pots or whale hide rings 40cm (16in) apart.
- Pot up the tomato plants into the bottomless pots using a good potting compost. Leave 2^1/$_2$cm (1in) unfilled to make watering easier.

Important: Check that the straw has not been treated with weed killer!

Soak the bale with water and pour 5 litres (1gal) of water over it every other day.

'Feed' the bale with a high nitrogen fertiliser twice each week. (Gardens Direct – ☎ 01992 441888 market a fertiliser specially for this purpose).

Note: the bale may heat up, take care not to plant up if it is too hot for the roots, that is over 30 ˚C (85 ˚F). If the straw feels warm, measure the temperature with a thermometer.

Tomato plants in a straw bale

- Water and care for as described but, in addition to watering the pots, soak the material upon which they are standing.
- After the first truss has set, feed the plants with liquid tomato fertiliser on the top of the compost only. Fertiliser watered onto the sand will drain away and be wasted.

Straw Bales

Three weeks or so before tomatoes are ready for planting, obtain rectangular straw bales (wheat is best) and position them in the polytunnel.

Make two holes in the bale with a sharp knife (not easy!) each large enough to take the tomato root ball.

Remove the pots from the tomato plants and place one in each hole. An alternative is to remove the bottom of the pots and sit them on the bale.

Care for as described.

Keep the bale watered and after the first truss is set, feed each week with tomato fertiliser.

Support each plant by tying to a garden cane which has been firmly pushed into the straw bale.

Tomatoes and sweetcorn

Chapter Five

Vegetables

Chicons grown in the polytunnel in October. The roots are raised outside during the summer, lifted and forced in complete darkness in autumn. A good lettuce substitute

There are two ways of using a polytunnel to produce vegetable crops normally grown outside. One is to grow the crop to maturity in a soil bed in the polytunnel and the other is to raise the plants in the polytunnel and transplant outside later.

Many of the 'outside' vegetables will succeed in a polytunnel and there are advantages of growing them there. The most obvious advantage is early crops, new potatoes in April, spring sown cabbages, cauliflowers, peas, carrots and spinach in May/June – the period when home-grown vegetables are in very short supply. There is the added advantage that the usual pests are absent and the crops are young, tender and blemish free. The early vegetable crops are harvested in plenty of time to allow tomatoes, cucumbers, melons, aubergines, maize, etc to be grown in the same soil.

In the depths of winter temperatures and light levels are too low to grow vegetables. A good rule of thumb is to sow or plant 6 weeks earlier than the usual date for sowing outside. The suggested planting times given here are for the Midlands. Other parts of the country will have earlier or later dates dependant upon the local climate.

Crops grown to maturity in soil beds:

- Cabbage (hispi)
- Carrot (early variety)
- Cauliflower (early crop)
- Climbing French bean (early crop – very susceptible to red spider mite)
- Courgette (needs a lot of space)
- Endive (late crop, very hardy)
- Land cress (early and/or late crop)
- Lettuce (early and late crop, grow outside in summer)
- Pea (sow first early wrinkled seed)
- Potato (early)
- Radish (early – will not succeed if too warm)
- Spinach (early crop)
- Spring onion (sow autumn for an early spring crop)
- Sweet corn (good crop to follow early potatoes)

USING THE SOIL BEDS

Spinach

Early February

- Select a summer variety not spinach beet nor New Zealand spinach.
- Rake the bed level and sprinkle seeds thinly and evenly over the whole area.
- Water well and cover with a fleece.
- After germination, which will be rather slow, hand weed where necessary.

- When the crop is growing well remove the fleece and give a single feed of liquid fertiliser.
- Harvest the leaves as required. Leave two or three leaves on each plant to encourage rapid regrowth.

Climbing French beans, raised in root trainers and planted in a soil bed. These take little space and produce a very large crop

Carrots

Early February

Carrots are a wonderful crop to grow in a polytunnel and they are free of carrot fly! A good variety for early production and flavour is the round carrot, Parabell. The traditional shaped variety, Amsterdam Forcing, is a little later, but crops very well in a polytunnel. Better yields are obtained by broadcasting the seeds instead of sowing in rows.

- Rake the soil to a fine tilth.
- Sprinkle seeds as evenly and thinly as possible over the soil.
- Rake over once more very lightly to cover the seeds.
- Water, using a watering can with a fine rose.
- Cover with a layer of fleece.
- After 2 to 3 weeks remove the fleece and hand weed by pulling out any seedling which is not a carrot. Once the carrots have their fourth leaf they will smother any other weeds that germinate.
- Water the carrots with care as too much water will produce leaves instead of roots. Use a haws can (or a hosepipe with very low pressure) and apply the water directly to the soil – if the foliage gets very wet it will collapse.
- In June the first carrots will be large enough for pulling.

If the soil is very weedy, do not broadcast but sow in rows. Cut slits 6in (15 cm) apart in the soil with a spade and fill them with multi-purpose compost. Sow the carrot seeds thinly in the compost. The weeds that do grow will be in-between the rows and can be controlled more easily.
If there is any space available in late August – sow an early variety of carrots and grow as described above. This crop should be ready for harvest in January.

Polytunnel grown carrots are ready in May

Cabbage

Mid February

Hispi cabbage in April

Hispi is the earliest spring sown variety. It has an excellent flavour but the hearts begin to split within a week of becoming firm – do not grow too many.

- Sow Hispi cabbage in root trainers filled with multi-purpose compost (see page 41/42). Place one seed in each section and germinate in a propagator.
- Transfer to the bench and grow on until the fifth leaf stage.
- Transplant into a soil bed in rows 22½cm (9in) apart. Firm the soil around each plant.
- Keep well watered. When the plants are growing away give a liquid feed.
- Harvest alternate plants to use as spring cabbage and leave the others to heart.

Cauliflower

Mid-February

The secret of good cauliflowers is to grow them without a check. A polytunnel provides the ideal environment for an early crop. There are many varieties of early cauliflowers, 'King', 'Montano', 'All the Year Round' and 'Snowball' all perform very well in a polytunnel.

- Raise an early variety of cauliflower plants in the same way as Hispi cabbage.
- When the plants reach the five leaf stage (but before the stem is the thickness of a pencil) transplant into the soil bed. Cauliflowers tend to become ready for harvesting at the same time and frozen cauliflowers are not as nice as fresh ones. The cropping period can be increased from a single sowing by planting out the bed in two halves, with one week between the plantings. The extra week the plants spend in root trainers delays their maturity.
- Space the plants 20x20in (50x50cm) apart. This spacing will produce medium sized curds. If larger curds are required, increase the planting distance.
- Keep well watered and give a liquid feed every 2 weeks – Phostrogen, Sangral or Miraclegro.
- Harvest as soon as ready – a cauliflower does not remain in good condition on the plant for more than 2 or 3 days. Bending leaves over the developing curd may increase its life for a few days.
- Pull up the plants as soon as harvest is complete.

Peas

Mid-February

For really early peas select a variety such as Hurst Beagle.

- Sow the seeds individually in root trainers, using a multi-purpose compost.
- Place in a propagator (or a warm room) until they have germinated.
- Transfer to a bench in the tunnel to grow on.
- Keep an eye on the roots (this is easily done by opening a root trainer) and when each plant has a good root system plant them out in a tunnel soil bed. If the soil has been manured no fertiliser will be needed.

Just a few weeks later the peas are ready for picking

- Plant a triple row, with the rows 12cm (5in) apart with 10cm (4in) between each plant.
- Arrange a net 90cm (3ft) high for the peas to climb.
- Water sparingly. When the first flowers appear increase the amount of water and keep the soil moist.
- Harvest the pods as they become full taking care not to disturb the plants.
- As soon as the crop has been harvested, remove it and plant a summer crop such as sweetcorn.
- You will not find any maggots in the peas as they will be harvested before the pea moths emerge.

Row of peas just transplanted from root trainers

Potatoes

Mid-February

An early potato is one that matures quickly. There are many varieties to choose from. Maris Bard is a good choice and reasonable sized tubers can be lifted at the end of April from a mid-February planting – providing the seeds were well chitted.

Maris Bard potatoes – just lift enough as tubers this young do not keep

Early potatoes being covered to protect from possible frost

- Purchase seed tubers in December or early January and keep them in a warm, light place until they have strong chits (shoots) about 3cm (1in) long.
- Before planting rake in 100g sq m (3oz sq yd) of Chempak No 4 (15:15:30) or a similar fertiliser.
- Plant the tubers buds upwards with 5cm (2in) of soil above. Allow 23cm (9in) between the tubers and 60cm (2ft) between the rows.
- As the plants grow, earth them up with soil from between the rows. This stops light from turning the new tubers green.
- Water regularly, keeping the soil moist but not wet.
- When frost is forecast, protect the plants by covering with fleece, sheets of newspaper or black plastic. If black plastic is used it must be removed during the day.

- Examine the developing tubers from time to time by scratching gently into the soil near to the base of a plant. When the tubers have reached the size of small marbles give a good watering – 22 litres sq m (4gal sq yd) to encourage growth.
- As soon as the plants have finished flowering the first tubers will be ready for harvest.
- Only dig up enough for immediate use, leave the others to grow. New potatoes are best eaten very fresh as the sugars in them begin to turn into starch soon after lifting.

Note: If a few of the new tubers are saved and planted in September there is a good chance of having new potatoes on Christmas Day.

Sweetcorn

Early April

It is possible to get sweetcorn over a long season by growing one crop in the polytunnel and a later crop outside. Both crops are raised from seeds sown in root trainers in the polytunnel. Most varieties of sweetcorn grow to over 2m (7ft) high in a polytunnel. If your polytunnel is lower than this use a dwarf variety.

- In early April sow sweetcorn seeds in deep root trainers (or individual pots) and germinate in a heated propagator. As soon as the seeds germinate, transfer to the polytunnel bench. Cover at night if there is any danger of frost. Sow a second lot in early May.
- Water and feed the plants regularly.
- As soon as space is available in a polytunnel bed, (i.e. after cabbage or potato harvest) rake 120g per sq m (3oz per sq yd) of growmore fertiliser.
- Plant out in a square pattern keeping the plants 30cm (12in) apart, both ways.
- Water regularly – if the leaf edges begin to roll up they are short of water. Give additional water when the male flower first appears and again whilst the cobs are swelling.
- When the silks (female flowers) begin to turn brown, peel back a small section of leaves from the cob and examine the seeds. If these are plump, soft and yellow the cob is ready.
- Grip the cob firmly and snap it off with a downward movement. The sooner the cob is eaten the nicer it will be. Cobs freeze very successfully.
- When the risk of frost is over, plant the second lot of sweetcorn plants outside.

Sweetcorn cob harvested 10 weeks after a crop of early potatoes

Sweetcorn ready for hardening off

Courgettes

Early April

A very large crop of courgettes can be obtained from a single plant. Inside a polytunnel these plants grow very large. It is therefore important to select a bush variety such as Ambassador.

- In mid-March sow seeds individually in 12½cm (5in) pots of multi-purpose compost.
- Germinate in a heated propagator.
- When the plants have their first true leaves, transfer to the polytunnel bench. Give additional protection in frosty weather.
- When the compost is full of roots (but not potbound) plant in the centre of a soil bed, 60cm (2ft) from the end. If planting two, allow 120cm (4ft) between the plants.
- Sink the plantpot alongside the rootball with the top level with the surface. When watering fill this pot with water several times.

When grown in a polytunnel a courgette plant produces a very large crop. Regular inspection is needed otherwise the courgettes soon become marrows

- Water regularly, if the bed has been properly pre-pared with plenty of organic matter the plants should not require feeding.
- During bright sunshine remove a fully open male flower, take off its petals and transfer pollen to the female by touching the flower centres together. This should only be necessary in polytunnels where insecticides are used.
- Harvest the courgettes by cutting through the stem with a sharp knife.

Caution! Harvest at least every third day as courgettes become marrows at an alarming rate.

Parsley

A continuous supply of this most useful plant is easily obtained. Two sowings are necessary, one to provide plants for growing outside and a second for a winter supply in the polytunnel.

There is always a spot for parsley with its attractive leaves – even in all flower gardens.

Parsley on a 'spare' corner of the polytunnel bed

Growing Parsley

Mid-February

- Select a variety with curled leaves – 'Darki' from Kings is excellent.
- Fill a half tray, divided into six sections, with multi-purpose compost and water it.
- Make five holes in each section about 1cm (½in) deep.
- Drop one seed into each hole – do not cover as parsley requires light to germinate.
- Place in a heated propagator until the seed leaves appear. This takes about 3 weeks.
- Transfer to the polytunnel bench and grow on until the plants have a third true leaf.
- Harden off, remove the six blocks of plants and, taking care not to disturb the root balls, plant outside with 15cm (6in) between the blocks.

July

- Raise a second batch of plants in a similar way.
- Plant up in a polytunnel bed.
- *To harvest:* pick individual leaves as required, always leave three or four leaves on each plant to speed up the growth of new ones.
- The first planting can be cropped all summer and autumn. The second planting will provide fresh parsley for the remainder of the year.

Note: Parsley is sometimes attacked by carrot root fly. If this is a problem in your garden – cover with fleece or insect netting.

SALAD CROPS

The polytunnel provides an excellent environment for salad crop production, both early in the year and later in the autumn. During the summer, salad crops are best grown outside – especially lettuce and radish as they do not tolerate very warm conditions.

Lettuce

Types of Lettuce

Butterhead

A heart forming type with soft, delicate leaves. Seeds of butterhead lettuce will not germinate at temperatures in excess of 24°C (78°F).

Crisphead

The leaves of crispheads are succulent, crisp and wrinkled. The hearts are usually larger than those of butterheads.

Cos

A cos lettuce forms an upright elongated heart. The leaves are long, crisp and sweet. Some varieties of cos need tying with string around the top to encourage heart formation. Cos lettuces are slower to mature than the other types.

Loose leaf

These types do not form hearts and individual leaves can be picked as required. Most loose leaf varieties have soft, curled leaves but varieties (Frisby) are now available with crisp leaves.

Cos varieties of lettuce can also be grown as loose leaf types. Heart formation is prevented by very close planting.

Some varieties of lettuce have been bred for winter production. If these are sown in summer they will bolt without hearting.

In theory lettuce can be grown in a polytunnel all the year round. This seldom works in practice as there is almost no growth in winter and the various fungus diseases thrive in the humid conditions that often prevail. Endive is a good substitute. It is hardy and can be harvested well into the winter. Lettuce can be ready for harvesting in April – providing the correct variety is selected.

January

- Sow Novita and Kelleys in root trainers and germinate them in a propagator with a low setting.

Lollo Rosso and Lollo Bianco lettuce in a polytunnel bed

- Transfer to a bench and grow on – growth is rather slow due to low temperatures and light levels.
- When plants are large enough, transplant into a soil bed 30cm (12in) apart along rows that are also 30cm (12in) apart.
- Keep the soil moist and, when the plants are growing well, give a liquid feed.
- Harvest Novita by picking individual leaves and leave Kelleys to heart up.

For indoor lettuce to follow the first crop:

March

- Open drills in a soil bed 1cm (½in) deep in rows 30cm (12in) apart.
- Water the bottom of the drills.
- Sow seeds of a butterhead variety such as Avondefiance very thinly along the bottom of each drill. If loose leaf varieties are preferred sow Lollo Rosso and Lollo Biondio.
- Cover the seeds with a multipurpose compost.

Beetroot

Early March

Beetroot will stand a little frost and is an ideal crop for early production in a polytunnel.

The only real problem is that of 'bolting' ('bolt' = run to seed before forming a beetroot) but that has been largely overcome by plant breeding.

- Select an early bolt resistant variety. Boltardy is a good one, but there are others.

Cell grown beetroot ready for planting

- Sow *three seeds in each section of a divided tray using a seed compost.
- Germinate in a propagator.
- Beetroot seeds are actually clusters of seeds and more than three seedlings should appear in each section. Pull out the weakest seedlings leaving between three and six plants in each.
- Transfer the trays to the tunnel bench.
- Give a half-strength general purpose feed each week.

- Prepare a soil bed and rake in 1oz sq yd (30g sq m) Growmore or other general purpose fertiliser.
- When there are enough roots to hold the compost in a ball, gently remove the clumps of beetroot from the trays. Do not separate the plants nor disturb the ball of roots.
- Plant the clumps of beetroot plants in a line with 15cm (6in) between each clump. Water as necessary, pull up weeds as they appear.
- As the roots become big enough to eat, harvest the larger ones by gently rotating them between the fingers and thumb. This will free them without disturbing the others which are left to grow.
- Remove the tops by twisting them off.
- Further sowings can be made in a similar way for transplanting outside – sow in early April.

* Some beetroot seeds are now supplied as 'monogerm', that is each seed produces only one plant. Sow six monogerm seeds per segment.

- As soon as the seedlings are large enough to handle, thin them out to 30cm (12in) apart.
- Keep watered and give a weak liquid feed every 2 weeks.
- Harvest as the hearts form.

April

- Sow seeds of summer varieties in root trainers.
- When the plants are large enough, harden them off ready for planting outside.

Salad Onions

Late September

This crop is hardy and is easily grown to maturity in a polytunnel.

- Remove the remains of the summer crop from a soil bed.
- Fork over the bed and tread it firm.
- Rake to a fine tilth.
- Draw a number of trenches, 1cm (½in) deep and 75cm (3in) wide.
- Use a rose can to thoroughly wet the bottom of each trench.
- Sprinkle thinly and evenly seeds of a winter hardy variety. Ordinary White Lisbon may not succeed. Use winter hardy White Lisbon.
- Cover the seeds lightly by sprinkling a little compost over them.
- Keep moist, but not wet, throughout the winter.
- In early spring begin a weekly feed with a balanced plant food.
- Remove any weeds that appear.
- Pull the largest onions as required and leave the others to grow.

Salad onions take longer to come to maturity than most other salads, but they produce their crop over a longer period. It is possible to have salad onions ready with the first crop of lettuce by sowing a winter hardy crop. For succession the second crop of spring onions should be grown outside under cloches.

Land Cress (also known as American cress)

Early February

This salad crop is very similar in appearance and taste to watercress. It is very easy to grow in a polytunnel and makes a useful salad crop early in the year.

- In February, prepare a soil bed and rake it to a fine tilth.
- Make drills 1-2cm (½-1in) deep and 15cm (6in) apart.
- Water the bottom of each drill and sow thinly, about three seeds per centimetre (½ in). Cover the seeds lightly by raking the excess soil back into the drills.
- Water and keep weed free. When the plants are growing strongly add a little liquid fertiliser to the water each week.
- Harvest by removing the larger leaves from the plant at soil level and leave the smaller ones to grow.

Land cress – very easy to grow and an excellent substitute for watercress

Radish

Early March

Cool conditions are required for the successful production of radish and it should only be grown as a polytunnel crop in late winter and early spring. Select a variety like Cherry Belle or French Breakfast. Avoid the long varieties such as Icicle and the Spanish ones.

Grow radish in a similar way as described for American cress or grow them to maturity in a general purpose compost in a 15cm (6in) pot and about twenty, evenly spaced seeds.

Slug damage to pot grown radish, a smear of grease (or Vaseline) around the pot rim would have prevented this

Endive

End of August

Large plant pots with holes covered used for blanching endive

Endive is an annual that is grown for its leaves. These may be braised but are most often eaten raw in salads. Endive is more hardy than lettuce and an easy crop to grow. Planted out after the tomatoes have finished it provides a most useful salad in the early winter.

Extra care is needed if endive is to be transplanted successfully. Plants are therefore best raised individually in $12^1/_2$ cm (5in) pots. Riccia Pancallieri, with its curly toothed leaves and a prostrate habit is a good variety to grow.

Endive tied for blanching. The plant must be dry when tied and opened after two weeks to prevent rotting

- Sow two or three seeds in each pot during August.
- Thin seedlings to one plant per pot.
- When there is room in a bed, plant out in rows spaced 30cm (12½in) apart with the same distance between the plants.
- Once the plants become established give just one foliar feed to increase the yield. Phostrogen, Miraclegro or any other well-known brand is suitable.
- Keep well supplied with water.
- Unblanched endive is bitter and unpalatable so blanching is essential. Three weeks before harvest cover the centre with a 15cm (6in) plant pot, the holes of which have been covered and blacked-out with electricians' tape. The plants must be dry when covered otherwise the edges of the leaves may rot. Alternatively the whole plant can be tied with string in such a way that the outside leaves exclude light from the inner leaves. Only blanch one or two plants at a time, as the blanched plants soon begin to rot around the leaf edges.
- Blanched leaves are light cream colour, pick these as required.

Raising Plants For The Outside Production Of Vegetables And Salads

The best way to grow the vegetables listed below is to start them off in the polytunnel and then transplant outside. For earlier production sow 4-6 weeks earlier. Winter crops such as brussel sprouts must be sown at the same time as you would outside.

Beetroot	French bean
Broad bean	Leek
Brussels sprout	Lettuce
Cabbage	Marrow
Calabrese	Onion
Cauliflower	Pumpkin
Celeriac	Ridge cucumber
Celery	Runner bean
Courgette	Sprouting broccoli
Fennel (Florence)	Sweetcorn

The advantages of doing this include:

- The crop is earlier.
- The season is extended.
- Hand weeding is eliminated and general weed control is much easier.
- No crop thinning is needed.
- Some pests are more easily controlled.
- Damage from diseases such as 'clubroot' is much reduced.
- Fewer seeds are used.
- Hardy crops benefit just as much as the half hardy ones.
- The need for a seed-bed outside is eliminated.
- Soil has a longer time for warming before the crop is planted.

With the exception of parsnips almost all of the common vegetables benefit from being grown in this way. There are six simple steps:
1. Sow seeds singly in a multi-purpose compost in individual pots or in root trainers.
2. Germinate them in a heated propagator or in a warm room. This is most important, especially very early in the year, when even the seeds of hardy plant, such as broad beans, may rot.
3. As soon as the seeds are beginning to emerge transfer them to the polytunnel bench.
4. Water as required and protect from frost.
5. Three weeks before planting outside cover the soil with clear plastic to warm it up.
6. Two weeks before planting outside harden the plants off (including the hardy ones).

Onion seeds being converted into sets. Sow in trays at the very end of May, allow to dry off during September and keep until spring for planting

One of the best containers to grow them in is root trainers. Up to fifty plants can be raised in the space taken up by a single standard plant tray. Each plant is grown in its own cell and can be transplanted with virtually no root disturbance. An alternative is to sow into small square pots 9cm (3in) for large seeds and 7cm (3 in) for

These runner beans will soon be ready for hardening off

Broad beans germinating in root trainers. They should be removed from the propagator as soon as they reach this stage

small seeds. Sow one (or at the most two) seeds in each so each cell or pot holds just one plant. Fewer seeds will be needed, the surplus can be kept until the following year – but not in the polytunnel – they need to be dry.

Brassicas (cabbages, cauliflowers, etc) grown in root trainers withstand clubroot and cabbage root fly much better than bare root transplants. The absence of root damage on transplanting helps to prevent cauliflowers from 'buttoning' (growing a very small cauliflower).

In order to have fresh broad beans over a longer period of time, sow half the seeds in root trainers in January and the other half in the soil in late March.

The half hardy vegetables such as French beans and runner beans crop for a longer season when started off in the polytunnel. Sweetcorn is more likely to produce well-filled cobs – especially if planted out in a block instead of a row.

This method of vegetable production is essential if very large onions are needed. The world champion large onion was grown to maturity in a polytunnel.

Chapter Six

Pests, Diseases and Disorders

Caterpillars on a Brompton stock, one of
the many pests which may be encountered
in a polytunnel

Plants are the ultimate providers of energy and materials for the whole of the animal kingdom. Plants in a polytunnel are no exception and many creatures will enter for a free lunch. The vast majority of creatures live their lives without troubling us, but there are a few that become a nuisance – these we call pests. Polytunnel growers do not see some of the common pests, but they do see the usual greenhouse pests. The pests and diseases dealt with in this chapter are the ones that are most likely to cause problems inside a polytunnel.

Chemical

Pest and disease control by chemical sprays has helped to increase the world's food production. If all chemical sprays were withdrawn from agriculture tomorrow there would be starvation on a massive scale.

Chemical sprays can cause problems, especially if used incorrectly – these include:
- Beneficial creatures may be killed along with the pests.
- Loss of pollinators reduces yields.
- As chemicals pass through the food chain they become concentrated.
- A residue of poison may be left on edible crops.
- Sprays may affect the health of the person applying the chemical.
- Possible health problems for people working in chemical factories.
- Pests become resistant to the spray. Two serious polytunnel pests, such as whiteflies and red spider mites, are resistant to insecticides.
- Some plants may be damaged.

Some plants produce their own insecticides – pyrethrum is extracted from an African chrysanthemum (now manufactured chemically). A new insecticide has been found in a species of Calceolaria that grows in Chile. This chemical is being researched and it is hoped to produce an insecticide to which pests do not become resistant.

No specific chemicals are recommended here as those allowed are continually changing. Several pesticides that were considered safe and in common use only a few years ago are now withdrawn. It is possible to garden without them although there are times when a good fungicide is most helpful in a polytunnel.

Pest And Disease Control In A Polytunnel

Safe use of chemicals:
- Use them only as a very last resort.
- Read the label with care and follow instructions to the letter.
- Stick rigidly to the dilution that is recommended, no stronger but also no weaker.
- Never spray insecticides on open flowers – bees may be killed.
- Store carefully, locked and out of children's reach, not in direct sunlight and do not allow to freeze.
- Do not use the same sprayer for pesticides and weedkillers.

Part of the skill of producing plants and crops in a polytunnel is the recognition and control of pests and diseases. The best method of controlling them is good garden hygiene. Avoid introducing pests and diseases and work with nature. Pests do less damage if a large variety of plants is grown both inside and outside the polytunnel. A vigorous plant can afford to lose the odd piece of leaf or a drop of sap to a hungry pest and well grown plants are less susceptible to pests and diseases than poorly grown ones.

Clean all used pots thoroughly with a diluted garden disinfectant

- If a watering can is used for weed killers, label it in large letters and never use it for watering plants.
- Never store garden chemicals in household containers such as milk or lemonade bottles.
- Take extreme care not to pollute ponds or waterways – fish are very susceptible to many garden chemicals.
- Never pour unwanted chemicals down the drain. Hand them in at the local Domestic Waste Disposal Site.

Algae growing on the inside of the polytunnel is best treated with Armillatox. No need to brush, spray it on and a few days later the sheet will be clean. Take care not to get any spray on the plants. Products which contain sulphur or chlorine may affect the ultra violet inhibitor and damage the sheet

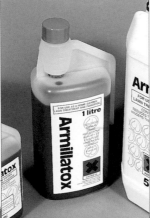

There are many chemicals available to assist control, but these are expensive and can do harm if misused. Use too much and useful insects such as bees and ladybirds may be killed, use too little and a strain of the pest appears which is resistant to the chemical. Chemical sprays should only be used when other methods have failed. It is illegal to use a chemical for a purpose which is not specified on the label.

Insecticide sprays and sticky insect traps kill (or catch) the good as well as the bad and it is best to manage without them. It is no use killing the greenfly if you also kill the hoverfly and the lacewing. The latest insecticides are more selective and those which contain pirimicarb will kill aphids and leave some of their enemies unharmed.

The author has never used an insecticide in a polytunnel. In the height of summer his polytunnel is alive with insects (and a resident toad), there is little plant damage and no problems with pollination.

Natural pest control is all very well when dealing with British pests but imported pests are a different problem as their natural enemies do not live in this country. These can be dealt with by using 'biological pest control' that involves introducing imported predators and/or parasites to keep the foreign pests under control. Some of our native pests can also be controlled by biological methods.

Several of the common garden pests are seldom seen in a polytunnel. Examples of these are carrot fly, cabbage root fly, pea moth, rabbits and pigeons.

Biological Control

Biological control makes use of the fact that most creatures in nature do not live until they die – they live until they are eaten. Biological control introduces creatures which eat pests – either from the inside (parasites) or from the outside (predators).

A polytunnel is an ideal place to use biological control. Enemies of troublesome pests are released into the tunnel. These enemies breed and keep the numbers of pests down to a level at which they do no real harm. Biological control organisms, complete with instructions, are dispatched by first class post. The instructions must be followed with care and the introduction made as soon as possible. All the available biological control creatures can be purchased from Defenders Limited (☎ 01233 813121). A different type of control creature is needed for each kind of pest. The creature that controls whitefly is no use against red spider mite and visa versa. Only purchase biological control organisms when the temperature is suitable for their release:

Hints on using biological control:

- Biological control is not a prevention, only use it if the pest is present.
- Order by telephone as soon as the temperature is high enough.
- Make a second (and third) introduction where recommended.
- Be patient, biological control is not a rapid process.
- Create humid and shaded areas to help the predators and parasites to become established.
- Monitor progress – use a hand lens to see some of the smaller creatures.

Pest	Control Organism	Minimum Temperature
Aphid	Aphidius (winged parasite)	18°C (64°F) (air)
Mealy bug	Cyptolaemus (predator ladybird)	20°C (68°F) (air)
Red spider mite	Phytoseiulus (predator mite)	10°C (50°F) (air)
Slug	Phasmarhabditis (nematode parasite)	5°C (41°F) (soil)
Soft scale	Metaphycus (parasite)	22°C (71°F) (air)
Vine weevil	Heterorhabditis (nematode parasite)	12°C (54°F) (soil)
Whitefly	Encarsia (winged parasite)	18°C (64°F) (air)

Introducing biological control parasites to control whitefly

This pack contains six million nematodes (tiny worms) which destroy slugs

Integrated Garden Care

Integrated Garden Care (IGC) is the best way of producing good crops with little loss to pests and diseases. This method uses a combination of all methods and all the available knowledge. It includes chemical control, but in a very limited way. Methods included in IGC are listed below:

1. Garden hygiene. Piles of old pots and boxes underneath the staging and elsewhere provide ideal conditions for slugs, woodlice, mice and other pests to spend their days in safety – and their nights feeding on your plants. Pots of dead plants may still contain the vine weevils that caused their death. Rubbish inside and outside the polytunnel may be producing fungus spores by the million. A tidy, well-organised garden with waste organic matter properly composted is the first step to pest and disease control.

2. Selection of varieties. More and more varieties are being bred with some resistance to disease. When ordering seeds, read the catalogues with care and select the varieties with inbred disease resistance.

3. Crop rotation. This is a tried and tested method of control that has been used with great success for hundreds of years. Practice this as far as possible both inside and outside the polytunnel.

4. Quarantine. When plants are brought into the garden check them very carefully. Look under the leaves for tiny eggs or scales and (if potted) tap them out of the pots and look for such pests as vine weevil grubs and the New Zealand flatworm. In addition to visual inspection, isolate the plants from the polytunnel for a couple of weeks. A very large plastic bag can be a useful way of doing this. After isolation repeat the inspection.

5. Sterile compost. Raise plants in sterile compost. This will ensure a disease free root system. Plants with good roots are more likely to withstand pest and disease attacks.

6. Diversity. Grow a range of different plants. Where only one type of plant is grown, pests and diseases are more difficult to control.

7. Encourage predators. Help birds, such as bluetits through the winter by regular feeding and keep them in the garden during spring by providing nest boxes. A small (fish free) pond, with a deep and a shallow area, will increase the numbers of frogs or toads. Grow 'insect' plants such as convolvulus tricolour to encourage hoverflies.

8. Insecticides. Use these only as a last resort and select the ones that are most specific to the target pest. Pirimicarb for example kills aphids but not ladybirds – providing it is used strictly in accordance with instructions.

9. Fungus diseases. Most of the troublesome plant diseases are caused by fungi. The best method of fungus control in the polytunnel is good ventilation. Systemic fungicides (those which are absorbed by the plant and move around inside it) can be very effective. Follow the instructions to the letter and don't soak the soil as it contains countless beneficial fungi.

10. Avoid methods that kill or catch everything. Yellow sticky traps may catch whitefly – but they also catch the tiny parasites which help to control them.

Applying biological control to cucumber leaves infected with red spider mites. The paper catches spillage for use on other leaves

11. Introduce biological control organisms into the polytunnel to deal with specific pests. It is now possible to control whitefly, red spider mites, vine weevils, slugs, aphids and mealy bug by this method. This list is growing.

12. Do not expect immediate results and be prepared to accept a little damage. Pests are controlled not made extinct – predators and parasites are on your side and they need something to live on!

Listed opposite are the symptoms of pests and diseases most common in British polytunnels. Several very common garden pests are not included as they seldom occur in polytunnels. Crops are in alphabetical order; locate the plant, find the symptom and then turn to the page that is numbered alongside.

Problems Common To Most Plants

To avoid repetition, these are not listed under the various crops.

Small insects, mostly wingless and usually in large numbers near to the buds and growing points, leaves sometimes sticky and turning black on upper surface	aphids page 106
Tiny white motionless 'insects' on lower parts of plants	aphids page 106
Leaves wilt, no other symptoms	drought page 114
Tips of stems – especially new growth wilts	drought page 114
Leaves with parts eaten, slime trails present	slugs page 108

Antirrhinum

Leaves – undersides with brown patches of fluffy growth	rust page 115
Leaves covered with a powdery white substance	powdery mildew page 112

Aubergine

Leaves with yellow spotting on upper surface, cobweb strands bridging leaves and stems with tiny mites crawling across. Older leaves dead and dry	red spider mite page 108

Bedding Plants

Leaves become bronzed or purple when planting out	not properly hardened off page 114
Seedlings narrow at base and die off in patches	damping off page 111
Plants at the edge of the tray small compared with those in the centre	insufficient water

Brompton Stock

Leaves with parts eaten, no slime trails	caterpillars page 106
Shoots at top begin to wilt and die, fluffy grey mould present	grey mould page 112

Cabbage & Cauliflower

Leaves with patches of grey and distorted growth, on close inspection the grey patch is seen to be a cluster of small insects	cabbage aphids page 106
Seedlings go thin at the base and fall over, usually in patches	damping off page 111
Young plants eaten off at ground level	cutworm page 107
Plants not thrifty, often seen wilting, roots with irregular swellings, no grubs present	clubroot page 111

Carrot

Roots split	splitting page 114
Outside of root rotten and dark purple or violet in colour	violet root rot page 113
Top of roots eaten, teeth marks visible	mice page 113
Large hole in root	cutworm page 107

Chrysanthemum

Flowers with fluffy grey mould, 'smokes' when tapped	grey mould page 112
Flowers with white flecks, small, narrow bodied, wingless insects crawling over plants	thrips page 109

Flower petals with brown, 'watery' patches	frost
Leaves – undersides with brown patches of fluffy growth	rust page 115
Leaves covered with a powdery white substance	powdery mildew page 112
Leaves with white, snake-like patterns	leaf miner page 107
Leaves sticky often turning black, white insects fly when the plant is disturbed. Small white scales on underside of leaves	whitefly page 110

Courgette

Leaves sticky, often turning black, white insects fly when the plant is disturbed. Small white scales on underside of leaves	whitefly page 110
Leaves with yellow spotting on upper surface, cobweb strands bridging leaves and stems with tiny mites crawling across. Older leaves dead and dry	red spider mite page 108
Leaves and sometimes fruit, covered with a powdery white substance	powdery mildew page 112
Fruit club shape with blossom end thin	pollination page 115

Cucumber

Leaves with yellow spotting on upper surface, cobweb strands bridging leaves and stems with tiny mites crawling across. Older leaves dead and dry	red spider mite page 108
Leaves sticky, sometimes turning black. Small white flies take to the air when the plant is disturbed. Scales on the underside of leaves	whitefly page 110

Leaves turning brown at the edges	too hot page 115
Leaves and sometimes fruit, covered with a powdery white substance	powdery mildew page 112
Stem blackened at the base and beginning to rot	stem rot page 113
Leaves distorted with yellow mosaic patterns	virus page 113

French Bean

Leaves with yellow spotting on upper surface, cobweb strands bridging leaves and stems with tiny mites crawling across. Older leaves dead and dry	red spider mite page 108
Leaves wilting, bottom of stem turning black and rotting	foot rot page 112

Fuchsia

Leaves sticky, sometimes turning black. Small white flies take to the air when the plant is disturbed. Scales on the underside of leaves	whitefly page 110
Leaves with yellow spotting on upper surface, cobweb strands bridging leaves and stems with tiny mites crawling across. Older leaves dead and dry	red spider mite page 108
Shoots – young shoots die from loss of a ring of bark	vine weevil page 110
Leaves - holes and notches of various shapes and sizes. 'C' shaped white, legless grub at the roots	vine weevil page 110

Grape

Fruit rotting with a grey mould between grapes	grey mould page 112

Leaves with yellow spotting on top and white mould underneath	downy mildew page 112
Leaves with yellow spotting on upper surface, cobweb strands bridging leaves and stems with tiny mites crawling across. Older leaves dead and dry	red spider mite page 108
Leaves with irregular lumps on the underside which contain a watery liquid	oedema page 114
Stems have clusters of small insects covered with white powder	mealy bug page 107

Lettuce

Plants grow suddenly tall	bolting page 114
Plants not growing well, 'sickly appearance', small white insects on roots	root aphids page 106
Leaves develop brown edges	tip burn page 115
Leaves rot, patches of dark mouldy growth	grey mould page 112
Stems rot off at soil level, brown markings	grey mould page 112

Melon

Melons are related to cucumbers and tend to have the same problems with similar symptoms

Pepper

Fruit has dark, rotting area at the base	blossom end rot page 113
Leaves with yellow spotting on upper surface, cobweb strands bridging leaves and stems with tiny mites crawling across. Older leaves dead and dry	red spider mite page 108

Leaves with distortion and mottling	virus page 113

Pea

Seeds dug up and eaten	mice page 113
Shoots eaten as they emerge	slugs page 108
Pods rotting with fluffy grey mould present	grey mould page 112
Leaves and sometimes fruit, covered with a powdery white substance	powdery mildew page 112
Seedlings narrow at base and die off in patches	damping-off page 111

Potato

Leaves roll and wilt, bottom of stem black and slimy, tubers soft and rotten	black leg page 111
Tubers have small round holes, tough yellow insect larva present. Only likely in year two and three following grass	wireworm page 111
Tubers green in colour	light
Tubers soft and spongy or tubers split or hollow	drought page 114
Tubers have brown scabby patches on skin	scab page 112

Spinach

Leaves with pale spots on upper surface, grey mould growth underneath	downy mildew page 112
Leaves yellow (young ones first) become distorted and small outer leaves wilt	virus page 113

Spring Onion

Bulbs rot at base, usually in groups, white mould present	white rot page 113

Sweetcorn

Cobs do not develop, white stripes on leaves	boron deficiency page 115

Tomato

Fruit splitting	splitting page 114
Fruit has dark, rotting area at the base	blossom end rot page 113
Fruit has hard unripe green patches when the remainder is ripe	too hot page 115
Flowers do not set fruit	pollination page 115
Leaves sticky, sometimes turning black. Small white flies take to the air when the plant is disturbed. Scales on the underside of leaves	whitefly page 110
Leaves with yellowing between the veins (old, shaded leaves nearly always become like this)	magnesium deficiency page 114
Young plants stunted with bluish tinge to foliage	cold page 114

Sweet Pea

Leaves with yellow spots on the upper surface and fluffy mould growth below.	downy mildew page 112
Leaves with parts eaten, slime trails present	slugs page 108

Sweet William

Leaves with light brown areas of fungus	rust page 115

Aphids (Also Called Blight, Greenfly And Blackfly)

Aphids are small insects which breed at an alarming rate. They feed by sucking plant juices; this makes the plants sticky and deprives them of the materials needed for growth. In addition, when aphids move from plant to plant they spread virus diseases in a similar way in which mosquitoes spread malaria in people.

There are many different types of aphids and the aphid that affects cucumbers is different from the one that affects busy Lizzies. Aphids are possibly the most troublesome pests in a polytunnel. Most aphids are wingless but, when a plant becomes crowded, winged females are produced and these fly to other plants. Almost every plant is liable to become infested by one of the 700 aphid species. Fortunately the aphid has lots of natural enemies, birds, beetles, ladybirds and their larvae, hoverfly larvae and lacewing

Cabbage aphids

larvae. There are also small insects that are parasites of aphids and fungus diseases which kill them. If no insecticides are used, the polytunnel aphid is not a nuisance during summer – the predators see to that. However in late winter and early spring the aphid is breeding rapidly and the weather is too cold for most of its predators.

Controlling Aphids

- encourage aphids' predators and parasites by not using insecticides or yellow sticky traps.
- keep a sharp lookout for aphids (the white skins they shed often give them away). Where only a few are present they can be dealt with by squeezing between finger and thumb.
- use a pressure spray to direct a jet of horticultural soap and water onto the colonies, this will wash most of them off. Repeat a few days later.
- if all else fails use a systemic insecticide with an active ingredient specific to aphids. Systemic insecticides tend to move upwards; it is therefore better to spray the lower leaves even though the aphids are near to the tops of the plants.

Caterpillars

Caterpillars are the larvae of butterflies and moths. They have strong mouth parts and are voracious feeders on plant tissue. There are several thousand species of which only a very few are likely to be seen in a polytunnel. These include the Tomato Moth and the four types of Cabbage Caterpillars. In addition to cabbages the latter feed on stocks and nasturtiums.

Control

- Keep a sharp lookout for eggs under the leaves – crush any you find.
- Hand-pick from the plants, picking off small ones is more effective than picking off the large ones which have already done the damage.
- Spray with 'Bactospeine'. This is a bacterium that causes disease in caterpillars. It is effective but rather slow acting.
- Spray with an insecticide that contains permethrin e.g. Picket.

Cabbage caterpillars on brompton stocks in the polytunnel

Cutworm

Cutworms are the larvae of moths. They are a drab grey/brown colour and live in the top few centimetres of the soil. They feed at night, damaging young plants by eating through the stems at ground level. In a polytunnel cutworms are only found in very small numbers. However a single individual can do considerable damage by working along a row of young transplants.

Control

• Searching the soil near to a damaged plant will usually find the culprit which can then be destroyed.
• Keep soil weed free – moths are more likely to lay eggs amongst weeds than on bare soil.

Leaf Miner

The adult females make tiny white spots on the leaves as they make holes in which to lay their eggs. The larvae hatch from the eggs and live between the upper and lower surfaces of the leaf. As a larva feeds it leaves a snake-like track through the leaf. Several species of plants are affected, damage is most often seen on chrysanthemums.

The snake-like markings on the leaves of this chrysanthem are the result of damage by leaf miners.

Control

• Remove and destroy infected leaves.
• Control weeds – especially groundsel.
• If many leaves are affected spray with an insecticide and repeat 2 weeks later.

Mealy Bug

The mealy bug is a little larger than an aphid, but it feeds in a similar way. Colonies of mealy bugs are covered with white fibres and a white powder. Many polytunnel plants are subject to attack; this leaves a weakened plant, covered in sticky honeydew in which a black sooty mould grows. Batches of eggs, a hundred at a time, are also covered with a protective white powdery coating.

The long tailed mealy bug

Control – Extremely Difficult!

• Remove as many as possible by playing a strong jet of water on them.
• Brush off with a paintbrush – preferably dipped in an insecticide.
• After removing as many as possible, spray with a systemic insecticide.
• Purchase biological control ladybirds (Cryptolaemus) which feed upon mealy bugs. The larvae of this ladybird also feed on mealy bugs, they are bigger than their parents and eat a good deal more.

Cryptolaemus, an imported ladybird which feeds on mealy bugs

Red Spider Mite

Red spider mites are an extremely serious poly-tunnel pest. Mites are very difficult to see on a leaf without the aid of a magnifying glass, but are more easily seen on their fine webs as they travel from one leaf to another. Mites hibernate in and around the polytunnel throughout the winter in large numbers; an infection one year will be followed by an infection the following year. Mites feed by sucking sap

These tiny spots on the cucumber leaf are caused by red spider mites feeding on the underside

from the leaves; this causes tiny yellow spotting on the upper surface. As infestation increases, the leaf turns yellow, hard and covered with fine cobwebs.

Red spider mites are resistant to many chemical sprays and this makes their control very difficult.

They damage plants in the following ways:

- weaken the plant by removing sap.
- yellow spots on the upper leaf surfaces.
- plants become covered with webs, cutting off light and preventing air movement.
- older leaves turn yellow and brittle.
- the plant often dies.

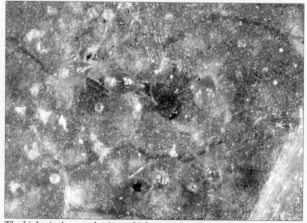

The biological control mites which eat red spiders

Control

- Learn to recognise the mites – use a hand lens.
- As soon as yellow specks are seen on the upper surface of leaves, examine the lower surface for mites. The yellow spots may have a different cause.
- Control weeds and rubbish both inside and around the outside of the polytunnel.
- Be very thorough when cleaning in autumn, use a garden disinfectant.
- If your polytunnel is mite-free take extreme care not to introduce mites with new plants.
- Spray susceptible plants with clean water as often as possible. Mites thrive in hot, dry conditions but not in cooler, humid conditions.
- Spray with Fumite or Vitax aerosol.
- If mites are present purchase the biological control organism (Phytoseiulus). This organism is also a mite. It feeds on red spiders and once it begins to breed, will give good control throughout the summer.

Although the red spider has a large range of host plants it is much more likely to infest some than others. Climbing French bean is very susceptible and is often cropping before the temperature is high enough for biological control to succeed. If red spiders are seen on French beans it may be wisest to remove the entire crop.

Cucumber is also a favourite target for red spider. By this time the temperature is higher and a combination of biological control and misting with water will usually give sufficient control to obtain a worthwhile crop.

Slugs And Snails

These are one of the most difficult pests; there are several species some of which live entirely under the soil. They feed by rasping the vegetation away with a special 'tongue' that acts like a file. They shelter during the day and feed at night. They remain active throughout the year and feed whenever the temperature is above freezing. Slugs and snails lay eggs in clusters of ten to thirty in soil cavities.

Thrips

Small brown insects with long narrow bodies 3mm long can be seen walking over the flowers. Many are wingless and they feed by tearing away small amounts of plant tissue. This leaves white streaks and flecks on flowers and leaves. Seedlings are sometimes killed by thrips.

Control

- Increase the humidity by extra damping down.
- Spray with a contact insecticide.

The pale markings on the petals of this flower are the result of damage by thrips

Half beer and half water in a sunken plastic cup makes an excellent slug trap

Slug on melon

Control

- Traps consisting of half beer and half water set at soil level will drown many slugs although the largest species can crawl out of these.

- Good garden hygiene reduces overall populations. A tidy garden and polytunnel have fewer places for them to hide from predators.
- Encouraging frogs and toads into the garden with a small pond providing both deep and shallow areas. This is a long term method that can be very effective – especially if the temptation to introduce fish is resisted.
- Poison slug baits laid strictly in accordance with the manufacturers' instructions will kill hundreds especially on a damp night. (Extra care must be taken as some baits are poisonous to animals and birds).
- Slugs often crawl on the inside of the plastic sheet at night. They can easily be picked off with the aid of a torch.
- Biological control is available in the form of a pack which contains some 6,000,000 nematodes – 'Nemaslug' from Defenders Ltd (☎ 01233 813121).
- Nemaslug is diluted and watered onto the plants and soil. The nematodes enter the slugs and breed; the slugs stop feeding and eventually die. This gives protection for about 6 weeks. After this time the nematodes disperse and slugs move into the cleared area from the untreated soil. Nemaslug is most effective on light soils and least effective on heavy clay soils.

Whitefly

A common pest in the polytunnel is a small white fly only 2mm ($^1/_{16}$ in) long. It spends most of its time underneath the leaves but flies off when disturbed. Its larvae are also white and they can be seen as scales on the underside of the leaf. Both adults and larvae feed by sucking sap from the plant.

The skins that fall from aphids are sometimes mistaken for whiteflies. The fact that the adults take off when disturbed is a good way to recognise this pest. The brassica whitefly is similar in appearance to the polytunnel whitefly. It is however a different species and will not attack polytunnel plants. Whitefly eggs and scales are resistant to most insecticides. Spraying with insecticide will kill only the adults (and not all of those). Systemic insecticides give better control – but on food crops?

Whiteflies damage plants in the following ways:
- weakens them by removing sap.
- makes them sticky with honeydew.
- makes them black, as a sooty mould grows in the honeydew.

Control

- check any new plants before taking them into the polytunnel. Use a hand lens and look underneath the leaves for eggs and larvae (called 'scales').
- control weeds both inside and outside the polytunnel.
- introduce the biological control organism (Encarsia). This organism is a tiny parasitic wasp and, providing the temperature is not too low, is very successful. If the introduction is successful, black scales will be seen underneath the leaves, each of these black scales will become a dead whitefly and a new wasp.

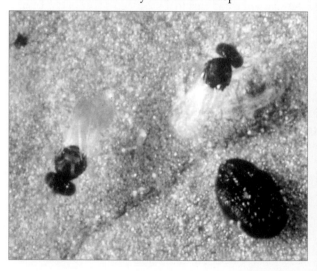

Encarsia. This tiny fly lays almost 100 eggs, one in each whitefly scale

Vine Weevil

A vine weevil is a small, brown, wingless beetle that hides by day and feeds on plant leaves at night. Eggs are laid in the compost, or soil and these hatch into creamy white larvae. The larvae feed on plant roots and cause very serious damage. Pot plants such as fuchsias, cyclamen, African violets, and begonias are very susceptible to vine weevils.

Vine weevils damage plants in the following ways:
- eats ragged areas around the edges of leaves, this is unsightly but much less serious than the root damage.
- The larvae eat roots, this causes sudden wilting and often death.

Vine weevil grubs

Wireworm

Wireworms are the larvae of click beetles. They have six tiny legs and are up to 2cm (1in) long, segmented, shiny yellow and tough skinned. Wireworms feed on the underground parts of plants. They burrow small round holes in potato tubers. Wireworms are only likely to be troublesome in a polytunnel for the first 2 years and then only if it is sited on an area of old turf.

Control

- Avoid growing root crops for the first 2 years after turf has been broken up for crops.
- Keep the soil weed free to discourage click beetles from laying their eggs.
- Before using home-made loam, check it for wireworms.

Black Leg

Black leg is the name given to bacterial diseases that cause the bottom of stems to blacken. In potatoes the rotting of the stems causes the smaller leaves to curl and yellow. The infection is transmitted from one season to the next by infected tubers rotting in store and infecting healthy tubers that may be used as 'seeds'.

Control

- Use certified potato seeds.
- Inspect seed potatoes before planting and reject any which are showing signs of rot.

Clubroot

Vegetables related to cabbages (not lettuce) and wallflowers and stocks are subject to this soil borne disease. The swellings on the roots interfere with water and nutrient uptake resulting in a very sickly plant. Once in the soil the organism which causes the disease lives for many years.

Control

- The only effective control is to avoid introducing the disease by crop rotation and raising transplants in sterile compost.
- Check pH regularly and lime when necessary – especially before planting a susceptible crop.
- Raise plants individually in pots or root trainers and do not use bare root transplants.

Damping Off

This is a very common disease caused by a soil borne fungus. Seedlings can damp off both before and after emergence, the latter being most common. Seedlings collapse and the fungus grows in them producing a mouldy appearance and a lot of spores.

Control

- Use sterile trays and compost.
- Sow seeds thinly.
- Maintain the best temperature to ensure rapid germination.
- Water sparingly.
- Treat with Cheshunt compound.

Control

- Remove any debris which could harbour adult weevils.
- Knock out any suddenly wilting plant and examine the compost for larvae.
- Drench the compost with bioHexyl.
- Purchase the biological control organism.
- The biological control organism is very successful. It is a microscopic worm that enters a larva, kills it with a bacterium and then feeds on it. The worm requires a temperature of 14°C (58°F) and can only work when weevil grubs are present. The preparation that contains the worms is available by post from Defenders Ltd and called NemasysH.

Adult vine weevil. These weevils hide by day and feed at night

Downy Mildew

This fungus disease penetrates the plant tissue much more deeply than the unrelated powdery mildew. Spinach develops the distinctive symptoms of yellow patches on the top of the leaves with a darker mould growth directly underneath.

Control

• Treat with Bordeaux Mixture or spray with a systemic fungicide. Do not harvest for at least 2 weeks after spraying.

Foot Rot

A soil borne fungus that attacks peas and beans. It usually enters through a wound and causes the base of the stem to blacken and rot and so kills the plant.

Control

• Remove and destroy infected plants.
• Avoid damage to the base of the stem, hand weed rather than hoe near to the plant.
• Raise plants in sterile compost and clean containers.
• Check pH of soil and correct where necessary.
• Rotate crops.
• Where water is held in butts, clean them regularly.

Powdery Mildew

This fungus disease is most often seen on the leaves of chrysanthemums, cucumbers, vines and courgettes. It is most likely to occur in hot, dry conditions especially where plants are crowded close together. The leaves develop patches with a thin coat of a whitish powder, the patches join and very often the whole plant becomes covered.

Control

• Burn infected debris.
• Spray at fortnightly intervals with a fungicide – take care, some plants may become scorched!

Scab

Potato tubers develop ragged, corky patches on the skin.

Control

• Grow the year before lime needs to be applied.
• Give a thorough soaking (5gal sq yd) when tubers are first forming.
• Do not compost the peelings from scabby potatoes.

Grey Mould

This is very common in polytunnels and infects a large range of plants. It occurs most often in autumn and winter when the atmosphere is damp and cool. Infected parts die back and become covered with a grey, fluffy mould which 'smokes' when disturbed due to the release of millions of spores.

Control

• Practice good garden hygiene to keep the numbers of spores as low as possible, remove and burn any infected material.
• Maximum possible ventilation – especially on damp days.
• As a last resort a systemic fungicide may be used. Too much reliance on fungicides may lead to the emergence of a strain of the disease that is resistant to the fungicide being applied.

Grey mould on brompton stock

Stem Rot

Several different diseases which attack stems are called 'stem rot'. In cucumbers the rot often occurs at the base and the plant wilts and dies.

Control

- When watering, avoid leaving a pool of water around the base of the stem.
- Pile compost around the bottom of the stem, this will soon become filled with roots. This method can sometimes cure a plant – providing the symptoms are seen at a very early stage.

Violet Root Rot

Carrot roots covered with a purple slimy substance to which soil clings. The carrot skin appears rotted and messy. Whole groups of carrots are often affected.

Control

- Burn all infected plants, together with any weeds growing alongside.
- Do not grow root crops in the infected bed for 4 years.
- Check that the bed is well drained, if not dig a soakaway at one end.

White Rot

Patches of spring onions wilt. On inspection the roots are seen to have rotted off and a white fungus is growing at the base of the bulbs. A magnifying glass reveals black specks amongst the white fibres. The fungus remains in the soil for many years.

Control

- Crop rotation.
- Dig out and remove infected soil and replace with fresh soil.

Virus

There are very many virus diseases that affect plants. The most likely one to be seen in a polytunnel is Cucumber Mosaic Virus which affects a very wide range of plants including dahlias, begonias, primulas, spinach, tomatoes and many common weeds. The symptoms vary with the species infected. The most common are yellow mosaic patterns which begin on young leaves and then spread to the older leaves. Growth is reduced or stopped and secondary infections may result in the death of the plant. Virus is spread from plant to plant by aphids, some types may be spread by knives or even hands.

Control

- Prevention, not cure is the only control.
- Keep aphid numbers as low as possible.
- Control weeds.

Mice

Mice can become a nuisance in a polytunnel by eating bulbs and seeds – especially peas and French beans. They dig up the seeds as they germinate and leave the shoot on the surface. They also chew packets of seeds.

Control

- Any packets of seeds in a polytunnel should be in a lidded box.
- Set spring traps, baited with chocolate.
- Dip pea and bean seeds in paraffin before sowing.

Blossom End Rot

A very common disorder of tomatoes and sometimes peppers. The actual cause is a shortage of calcium. There is usually sufficient calcium in the soil or compost, the problem is that the plant cannot absorb it due to lack of water.

Control

- Thorough and regular watering.

Blossom end rot on tomato

Magnesium Deficiency

Leaves turn yellow whilst the leaf veins remain green. Older leaves affected first.

Control

• Maintain magnesium levels in the soil by using magnesium limestone when liming.

Oedema

Swellings on the leaves of a wide range of plants. This may occur in a polytunnel when a plant cannot evaporate sufficient water due to high humidity.

Control

• Increase ventilation.
• Take care not to get the soil or compost too wet.

Drought

Plants and young stems wilting and drooping. If the condition persists the plant dies.

Control

• Tend plants every day, especially in summer. Water where necessary.
• Set up automatic watering systems with drip irrigation and/or capillary beds.

Cold

The leaves of young plants become purple/bronze and growth stops.

Control

• In tomatoes sow later and/or keep in a heated propagator for additional time.
• Cover with horticultural fleece.
• In bedding plants, harden off with greater care.

Bolting

Lettuce, celeriac, celery, beetroot and other plants run to seed before producing the edible part. This is often caused by a period of cold, incorrect hardening off or by sowing too thickly.

Control

• Sow seeds thinly and thin out to correct distances.
• Sow later in the season.
• Do not harden off too soon.
• Harden off over a longer period of time. If the weather turns cold give the plants extra protection.

Splitting

Carrots, and potatoes, may split during growth. The cause is rapid growth following watering after a dry period. Thickly sown carrots may split lengthways as they are lifted.

Some varieties of tomatoes are prone to splitting as they ripen, especially when the fruit has developed slowly during cold weather, causing tough skin.

Tomatoes splitting

Control

• Increase water holding capacity of soil by good manuring.
• Water regularly.
• Always close the polytunnel at night to keep the temperature as high as possible.

Pollination

Poor pollination results in the failure of fruit to set. Some fruits partially set and become mis-shapen.

Control

- Plants with single sex flowers such as courgettes are easily hand-pollinated. During bright sunshine remove a fully open male flower, take off its petals and transfer pollen to the female by touching the flower centres together. Remove a second male flower, take off its petals, place it inside the female flower and leave it there.
- Tomatoes are self-fertile. A jet of water, directed at the flower truss, assists pollination.
- Reduce insecticide sprays (preferably to none). This increases the numbers of insects and makes pollination more likely.

Tip Burn

Lettuce leaves become scorched around the edges. Especially over the hearts.

Control

- Check that sufficient water is applied in hot weather.
- Do not apply more than the recommended amount of fertiliser.

Boron Deficiency

Young growing points blacken and die. Brown patches in cauliflower curds.

Rust

Yellow spots on the upper surface of the leaves with brown 'rusty' areas underneath. Rusty pustules on stems. Carnations often have rust on the flower calyx.

Control

- Reduce humidity by not damping down and giving maximum ventilation.
- Pick infected leaves and burn them.
- Select cuttings from healthy plants.

Too Hot

Very high temperatures can cause 'sun scorch' where parts of a leaf become papery thin and die. Tomato fruit does not ripen evenly, parts remain green and hard – a condition known as 'greenback'.

Control

- shade susceptible plants from direct sun with plastic shade or even newspaper.
- make sure that leaves do not touch plastic covers.
- with tomatoes do not take off too many bottom leaves. Leave those on which shade fruit from afternoon sun.

Control

- Rake Borax (3g per sq m), into the soil before planting.
- Repeat each year.

Reference

Biological Pest Control Organisms

Defenders Ltd
Wye
Ashford
Kent
TN25 5TQ
☎ 01233 813121

Rootrainers

Bernard Salt
Corner Farm
Walton on Trent
Swadlingcote
DE12 8LR
☎ 01283 716297

Jiffy7s by post
Johnson & Son Ltd
London Road
Boston
Lincolnshire
PER21 8AD
Freephone ☎ 0800 614323

StoneWool Cubes and Fertilisers

Growth Technology
Fremantle House
21-25 Priory Avenue
Taunton
Somerset
TA1 1XX
☎ 01823 325291

Fertilisers

Garden Direct
Geddings Road
Hoddesdon
Herts
EN11 0LR
☎ 01992 441888

Horticultural Fleece

Agralan
The Old Brickyard
Ashton Keynes
Swindon
SN6 6QR
☎ 01285 860015

Polytunnels

Citadel Products
32 St Andrews Crescent
Stratford Upon Avon
CU37 9QL
☎ 01789 297456

Northern Polytunnels
Green Road
Colne
Lancs
☎ 01282 870444

Ferryman Polytunnels
Bridge Road
Lapford
Crediton
Devon EX17 6AE

First Tunnels
63 Dixon Street
Barroford
Lancashire
BB9 8PL
☎ 01282 601253

Fordingbridge Ltd
Arundel Road
Fontwell
Arundel
West Sussex BN18 0SD
☎ 01243 554455

Keder Houses

C L M Fabrications
Newtown
Offenham
Evesham
WR11 5RZ

Solar Tunnels

Solar Tunnels
2 Melrose Place
Ashington
W. Sussex
RH20 3HH
☎ 01903 742615

Mist Units

Access Garden Products
Crick
Northampton
NN6 7XS
☎ 01788 822301

Simply Controls
139 The Commercial Centre
Picket Piece
Andover
Hampshire
SP11 6RU
☎ 01264 334805

Plant Foods

Levington Horticulture Ltd
Paper Mill Lane
Bramford
Ipswich
IP8 4BZ
☎ 01473 830492

Maxicrop International Ltd
Weldon Road
Corby
Northants
NN17 5US
☎ 01536 402182

Bio from PBI
Britannica House
Waltham Cross
Herts
EN8 7DY
☎ 01992 623691

Garden Direct
Geddings Road
Hoddesdon
Herts
EN11 0LR
☎ 01992 441888

Phostrogen Ltd
28 Parkway
Deeside Industrial Park
Deeside
Clwyd
CH5 2NS
☎ 01244 280800

Pelco Fertilisers Ltd
251 London Road East
Batheaston
Bath
BA1 7RL
☎ 01225 859962

Miracle Garden Care Ltd
Sailsbury House
Weyside Park
Cattshall Lane
Goldaming
Surrey, GU7 1XE
☎ 01483 410210

Plants by Post

(for tubs and baskets)
Hayloft Plants
Cooks Hill
Wick
Pershore
WR10 3PA
☎ 01386 561235

(for chrysanthemums)
Elm House Nursery
PO Box 25
Wisbech
PE13 2RR
☎ 01945 581511

Equipment for Polytunnels

Two Wests & Elliott
Unit 4
Carrwood Road
Sheepbridge Industrial Estate
Chesterfield
Derbyshire
S41 9RH
☎ 01246 451077

Seed Suppliers

Basically Seeds
Rebvale Business Park
Newmarket Road
Risby
Bury St Edmunds
Suffolk
IP28 6RD

Dobies Seeds
Broomhill Way
Torquay
Devon
TQ2 7QU
☎ 01803 616888

D T Brown & Co Ltd
Station Road
Poulton le Fylde
Lancashire
FY6 7HX
☎ 01253 882371

Chiltern Seeds
Bortree Stile
Ulverston
Cumbria
LA12 7PB
☎ 01229 584549

Johnsons Seeds
London Road
Boston
Lincolnshire
PE21 8AD
☎ 01205 365051

Kings Seeds
Monks Farm
Kelvedon
Essex
☎ 01376 570000

Marshalls Seeds
Freepost
Wisbech
Cambs
PE13 2BR
☎ 01945 583407

Miltons Seeds
3 Milton Avenue
Blackpool
Lancs
FY3 8LY

Mr Fothergill's
Kentford
Newmarket
CB8 7QB
☎ 01638 751887

Organic Gardening Catalogue
Coombelands House
Addlestone
Surrey
KT15 1HY
☎ 01932 820958

Seeds-by-Size
45 Couchfield
Boxmoor
Hemel Hempstead
Hertfordshire
HP1 1PA

Seymour's Selected Seeds
Abacus House
Station Yard
Needham Market
Suffolk
IP6 8AS
☎ 01449 721420

Suttons Seeds
Hele Road
Torquay
TQ2 7QJ
☎ 01803 614614

Thompson & Morgan
Poplar Lane
Ipswich
IP8 3BU
☎ 01473 688821

Unwins Seeds
Histon
Cambridge
CB4 4ZZ
☎ 01945 588 522

Wallis Seeds
Broads Green
Great Waltham
Chelmsford
Essex
CM3 1DS
☎ 01245 360413

Soil Warming Cables

Baxters Ltd
201-203 Cleethorpe Road
Grimsby
DN31 3BE
☎ 01472 343989

Thermoforce Ltd
Bentalls Complex
Heybridge
Maldon
Essex
CM9 7NW
☎ 011621 858797

Warrick Warming Cables
101 Sedlescombe
Road North
St Leonards on Sea
East Sussex
TN37 7EJ
☎ 01424 442485

Reference Books

The RHS Plant Finder
Lists over 60,000 plants, from alpines to trees, over 600 nurseries and where to obtain them. The lay gardener's 'bible', updated annually. A comprehensive section on plant names.

The Fruit & Vegetable Finder
Compiled by the Henry Doubleday Research Association. Lists sources of all commercially available vegetable varieties and lists more than 4,000 varieties and where you may find them. Draws on the Heritage Seed Library at The Henry Doubleday Research Asssoc., and the National Fruit Collection Brogdale.

Robinsons Greenhouse Gardening. – Bernard Salt.
A no-nonsense practical guide for all gardeners - a vital source of information for both the novice and the more experienced gardener.

Kings Sow and Grow Vegetables – Bernard Salt
A comprehensive guide for growing over fifty vegetables. Suitable for both organic and traditional gardeners.
'...thoroughly recommend this book as being value for money, and for its accessible, down-to-earth style'   The RHS

Glossary

annual	plant that grows from seed, flowers and dies in one growing season.
anti-fogging	treatment on a plastic sheet to make water drops coalesce into a film.
anti-hotspot tape	a strip of foam which sticks to polytunnel hoops to protect the plastic sheet.
biennial	plant which grows from seed, flowers the following year and then dies.
biological control	method of controlling pests by the introduction of an organism.
blanch	exclude light to make plant parts white instead of green.
blight	loose term used to mean aphid or (in some uses) a fungus disease.
body blanket	a sheet of aluminium foil used to prevent a person from losing heat.
bolt	run to seed instead of making growth.
brassica	member of the cabbage family.
broadcast	sow seeds evenly over an area of soil instead of organising them into rows.
buttoning	cauliflower plant producing a very small premature curd.
chill factor	temperature reduction caused by the wind.
cloche	low transparent structure to protect plants.
complete fertiliser	a fertiliser which contains nitrates, phosphates and potash.
compost	growing medium for plants in trays and pots.
damping down	wetting the polytunnel floor to increase humidity.
degradable	material which can be broken down by bacteria.
disbud	remove one or more flower buds.
drill	shallow trench in which seeds are sown.
eddy (eddies)	a small whirlpool of wind.
F1 hybrid	the first cross between two pure bred parents.
fertile soil	a soil which produces a good crop.
fertiliser	a substance which contains chemicals necessary for plant growth.
fleece	a non-woven fabric which admits light; used to protect plants.
floating mulch	a thin sheet of material which is supported only by the plants it is protecting.

foliar feeding	applying liquid fertiliser to a plant's leaves.
fungicide	a chemical substance which kills fungus.
fungus	large group of organisms which feed on organic matter whilst growing inside it.
glyphosate	a chemical which kills grass and other plants.
greenhouse effect	raising the temperature by letting in short wave radiation and preventing long wave radiation from leaving.
half hardy	plant which can grow outside but is killed by frost.
harden off	gradually acclimatise a polytunnel plant to outside conditions.
herbicide	chemical substance which kills plants.
hormone	a chemical, small amounts of which influence growth.
horticultural fleece	a non-woven fabric which transmits light: used to protect plants.
hydroponics	growing plants in a solution of nutrients instead of soil.
intercropping	growing a row of plants between the rows of an unrelated crop.
jiffy7	disc of peat contained in a nylon net to root a single cutting.
keder plastic	bubble sheeting made of an extremely strong transparent plastic.
lateral	side shoot or root.
micro-nutrient	a chemical which plants require in very small amounts.
micropore plastic	plastic sheet with very small perforations used to prevent plants from rooting into capillary matting.
module tray	a plastic tray with very small cells in which to raise seedlings.
monogerm	a seed which produces a single plant.
mulch	a layer of material placed on the soil surface.
multi-purpose compost	material which can be used in plant pots for sowing seeds or growing plants.
node	leaf joint on the stem.
perennial	a plant which lives for several years.
pH	the units by which the degree of acidity is measured.
phosphate	an element which is essential for plant growth.
pollination	the transfer of pollen from the male parts of a flower to the female parts of the same flower or another flower of the same species.
potash	an element which is essential for plant growth.
pot up	transfer a seedling or cutting to a pot.

predator	an animal which eats other animals.
prick out	transfer a seedling to a tray or pot.
propagate	raising new plants from seeds or cuttings.
rhizome	an underground stem.
ring culture	a method of growing tomatoes.
rooting medium	a substance into which cuttings are inserted to form roots.
rose	a fitting on a watering can spout to give a fine spray.
rosecan	watering can fitted with a rose.
rotation	a system which ensures that no crop is grown in the same area more often than one year in three.
seephose	a hosepipe with porous sides, laid on the soil to water plants along its length.
stonewool	fibrous material, made from rock, for plant propagation.
stop	remove the growing point from a shoot.
stopping	removal of the growing point from a shoot.
stools	the roots and lower buds of a plant all of which may, or may not, be below the soil surface.
succession	the availability of a crop over a long period.
tilth	the crumb structure on the soil surface.
trace element	a chemical which plants require in very small amounts.
true leaf	leaves which grow after the two seed leaves.
virus	an extremely small organism which can only exist in living things. It causes diseases in plants and animals.
water stress	reduction in plant growth caused by too little water.
woolmoss	a substitute for natural moss manufactured from wool.

Practical Points for Success

POLYTUNNELS

1 ☞ Before erecting the structure make sure that the base is perfectly rectangular by checking that the diagonals are exactly the same length.

2 ☞ Before applying the sheet:

a. Cover all sharp edges with tape.

b. Stick 'anti-hotspot' tape to all metal which will be in direct contact with the sheet.

3 ☞ Pull the sheet very taught along the ridge before fixing.

4 ☞ Fit double doors (or large opening vents) at both ends to give straight-through ventilation.

5 ☞ Place thick expanded polystyrene on the staging and cover with a sheet of plastic.

6 ☞ Organise the soil area into 1m (4ft) wide raised beds and never walk on the beds.

7 ☞ Dig a generous amount of garden compost or manure into the soil beds each year.

8 ☞ Practice crop rotation in soil beds. Where the cropping plan makes this impossible give a bed a year's rest by covering it with a black plastic mulch and placing growbags on top.

9 ☞ During damp autumn days give maximum ventilation to control fungus disease.

10 ☞ After watering the plants in summer, give the paths a good wetting to keep the humidity high.

11 ☞ Always close the tunnel at night to keep night-time temperatures as high as possible.

12 ☞ When cold nights are expected close the tunnel up well before sundown to get a layer of condensation on the sheet. this will freeze and give additional insulation.

13 ☞ On frosty nights cover tender plants with one or two layers of fleece. It will not blow away and the fleece will last for many years.

14 ☞ Keep the inside of the sheet free of algae. An occasional spray with a 1% solution of Armillatox will do this. Avoid getting any spray on the plants.

15 ☞ Do not allow sprays which contain sulphur or chlorine to come into contact with the plastic cover.

16 ☞ Do not sow or plant too early in the season. Four to six weeks earlier than outside is about right for most crops.

17 ☞ Check that the plants at both back and front of the staging are getting enough water.

18 ☞ If plants on capillary matting become too wet move them off the matting for a couple of days. Dry matting can be difficult to re-wet.

19 ☞ During spring and summer feed regularly – once each week at least – but don't overfeed.

20 ☞ Harden off all plants – even the hardy ones. Feed plants during the hardening off period and give a feed immediately before planting out.

21 ☞ Use Jiffy7s for cuttings.

22 ☞ Keep plenty of space between pot plants. As they grow larger move them apart.

23 ☞ Introduce biological control organisms as soon as the pest is seen. For whitefly control make three introductions of Encarsia over a period of 4 weeks.

24 ☞ Remove all plant debris as soon as a crop is finished.

CLOCHES

1 ☞ In spring position the cloches 2 weeks before sowing or planting.

2 ☞ Give increasing amounts of ventilation.

3 ☞ Choose a damp, sunless day for cloche removal.

Index

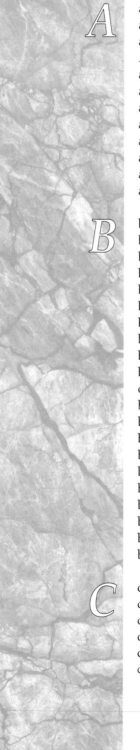

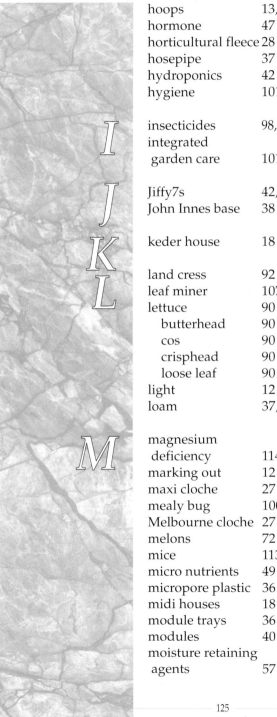

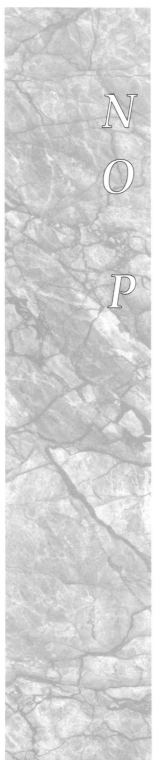